Why I Left the

Beth Axton

FAITHBUILDERS

British Library Cataloguing-in-Publication Data. A catalog record for this book is available from the British Library

ISBN: 9781912120277

Cover Design by Jem Butcher.

Printed in Great Britain in 2019. Printed and bound in Great Britain by Marston Book Services Limited, Oxfordshire.

I wish I knew how it would feel to be free
I wish I could break all the bonds holding me,
I wish I could say all the things I should say
Say 'em loud, say 'em clear for the whole world to hear.

I wish I could share all the love that's in my heart,
Remove all the doubts that keep us apart.
I wish you could know what it feels to be me
Then you'd see and agree that everyone should be free.

I wish I could give all I'm longing to give,
I wish I could live like I'm longing to live.
I wish I could do all the things that I could do
And though I'm way overdue I'd starting anew.

I wish I could be like a bird in the sky
How sweet it would be if I found I could fly.
I'd soar to the sun and look down on the sea
And I'd sing 'cause I'd know what it feels like to be free.

Dick Dallas
Permission applied for

Follow me
through 4 tumultous
years of fear and
deceit to Freedom
and happiness.
This book is a
page turner.
Best Wishes
Beth Axton
2025

Contents

Foreword

In her early adult life, Beth Axton was a woman hungry to know the truth. She initially sought it by joining a religious community known as the Unified Family (they became popularly referred to as the "Moonies," so-called after their founder, Rev. Sun Myung Moon). However, Beth slowly became disillusioned with its leaders and the austere way of life they advocated.

The Christian church initially held no appeal for Beth. Yet as time went on, Beth came to understand that the Lord Jesus Christ had been calling her, wanting her to open the door of her heart to him. Eventually, she found what she was looking for, by receiving Jesus Christ as her Lord and Saviour.

Some of us may find it hard to believe the testimony of deliverance from the dark powers which had driven her, but then that may well be because we have never encountered these things ourselves. Yet the result of that deliverance has been the glory Beth has brought to God, in a life spent serving the Lord Jesus Christ. Throughout this book, Beth emphasizes God's loving care and protection of her over many years.

I believe this book will be a blessing to anyone who is sincerely seeking God, whatever their current religious adherence We may all begin our journey of faith from different starting points, but I believe, as Beth does, that it is only in Jesus can we truly find the life and truth we crave.

Rev. Mathew Bartlett

Feeling Trapped

"How dare you disobey our authority. You have disobeyed divine authority and your very name is accursed. Do you think your ridiculous little life is of any value next to the Divine Master's? Whatever's going on in that damned head of yours?"

I stood utterly silent, pressing myself as hard as I could against the wall of the tiny room. I had never thought that I would be found out. Secretly, I had gone home for a few hours to see once again my parents whom I had denounced when I had joined The Unified Family. This is what made my group leader John* so incensed.

"Your parents have got absolutely no right to see you or know anything about you. Are you following Master or not?" The rage continued, the language progressively getting worse. I was a nothing. Of course, it was true in the light of what I had done. I should never have attempted to see my parents again, not now that my whole life was dedicated to the service of Sun Myung Moon. Whatever madness had taken me over?

"Get upstairs and make a decision – either get out now, be gone and be damned, or get your life 100% dedicated to Master! NOW GET OUT OF MY SIGHT." Like a terrified dog I made for the door and hurriedly went alone to the dismal shambles of an attic that about 15 of us girls lived in. There were no beds, we slept anywhere on the floor. I found a corner. Oh, what was I to do? What was I to do? The words pounded in my brain. The rage of shouting words had at last stopped but my own mind shouted as loud at myself. What a terrible, ridiculous situation I was in, and the most horrible part of it was that it felt to me like there was no escape.

What was I thinking of, to see my parents again? I had broken a divine law, and the day had been futile, and yet … and yet the most unexpected, incredible thing had happened. Could it really be true? And why …? What if …?

---

* Not his real name.

Forget it! John had been quite right to be enraged with me. There was only one solution, and that was to do obeisance to Sun Myung Moon, the Divine Master, and to completely dedicate my life anew to him. From now on nothing would stand in the way of my living a life of utter service to him, no matter what it cost. After all, my life is nothing, and he is everything; I must get things into proportion.

That dark, dreary, miserable and frightening day, I re-dedicated myself to Sun Myung Moon. How I wished with all my heart that I had never heard his name. Yes, I truly believed that he was the almighty, all-powerful god, who knew my every thought, and yet never had such fear and unhappiness flooded me. How had I ever got myself into this desperate situation? Crouching in the darkness, my mind tremblingly drifted back to only a few months ago when life was altogether different.

At 20 years old, I loved fashion clothes and the Top Ten music and thoroughly enjoyed my job as a secretary at the Atomic Energy Research Establishment at Culham Laboratory, Berkshire. I felt very privileged to be there and loved the wide spacious offices and the modern electric typewriters installed in my own office. The other office workers and I shared all our ideas over lunches in the beautiful staff restaurant and walked around the lovely gardens or sat on the wooden benches put out especially for us. In winter we chatted and talked over every subject that came into our heads in the soft armchairs of the coffee lounge amidst the tall tropical potted plants. Life was good and stress-free.

"You know we're really fortunate to be here," said Anne as we sat in the grounds one sunny day. "We've got good jobs, beautiful conditions, modern equipment and friendly people to work with. I don't think we could ask for anything more. It would be silly to ever leave somewhere like this. I think I might stay here until I retire!"

"Hmm," I mused, "I suppose I might do just the same." I already had some experience of working in another office. It had been drab and stuffy, and I recalled laboriously pushing down the keys of a heavy old black manual typewriter in a dim little room. There was nothing to do in the lunch time but eat sandwiches by myself over the dirty, old-fashioned, wooden desk. "Yes, life has everything it can offer here, oh, and by the way, are you coming to the dance on Saturday night – they say it's a really good band and those nice new accountants are coming!"

"Yes, sure I am – I'll see you there."

So what had happened? And why was I now in this dim little attic on a remote farm hating every moment of my life amongst strangers? Strangers who had already fleeced me of every penny until I felt helpless to escape!

Just what had happened in these last few months?

A Regrettable Encounter

It had started with a simple Christmas shopping expedition. In the midst of the usual chaotic crush there stood a young man shouting out in a loud voice, "Who will listen to the things of the Kingdom of God? Who will stand still in this rush of Christmas to listen to news of the Messiah? Where are you heading? Come, stop and listen." I admired the bold nerve of such a speaker and stopped for a few moments. In a second a strange young man was beside me pushing a leaflet into my hand and telling me that each one of us has a destiny in God and that our greatest purpose in life is to seek out this great calling by following the Messiah. I lightly agreed, saying that too many people leave Christ out of Christmas – after all, isn't it His birth we are celebrating? I was not quick enough to see the frown on the young man's face nor to pick up the strange reply: "We only worship the true Christ."

"Yes," I flustered, trying to remember my Christmas shopping list. "People follow too many false ideas these days."

"Is Boots still open?" I thought, "And I've still got to get to Woolworths."

"I see you are someone who is seeking after the truth."

"Oh, yes."

"You must come to one of our weekends. The divine truth is revealed. God is calling people to discover Himself and to come apart from the world. Look at everyone around us, this is utter mayhem."

I was longing to get back into that mayhem and quickly agreed to thinking about a weekend and made the fatal error of giving my telephone number and address. Looking back, I realise, that was a very big mistake. The young man at last released me. He could contact me now until I agreed to come.

Christmas came and my Dad gave me a surprise gift of a beautiful mustard yellow suitcase. Inside it had a shiny lining of red satin silk with ruched pockets at the side. All the clasps were gold. I loved it, but I wasn't happy. I kept getting phone calls and letters. "You must come to one of our weekends. You must hear divine truth. This is highly important."

I sensed all along that there was something a little strange here, but I just could not pin it down. None of my family liked the leaflets, but I was just twenty years old and had lived a sheltered life. A strange mixture of curiosity and risky adventure rose up in me and I decided to go. One reason was to stop these phone calls. If I went and didn't like it, that would finish it once and for all.

The Unified Family, Rowlane Farm, Reading. I had arrived – along with about fifteen other guests who had been relentlessly contacted in the same way that I had. And what a strange weekend it was, and I was never gladder than when it was over.

"Each one of us needs to discover himself in God. It is no accident that you are here, you have been brought here for purpose. Father has been drawing you to this point all your life." The lady speaking looked drawn and intense and seemed to stare into our eyes as if she could see a deeper meaning in us than we knew in ourselves.

I felt exceedingly uncomfortable the whole weekend. There was an uncanny atmosphere and I almost felt that the very air was electrifying. The young men and women who lived there were plainly utterly committed and never spoke unless they felt that what they were saying was divinely inspired. I still thought at this stage that this was a Christian community and was utterly bewildered as to why I should feel frightened just by being there.

On the last evening it was revealed to us that the Messiah had come and was walking amongst us now. He was Korean and his name was Sun Myung Moon. Together with his wife, Holy Mother of the Earth, he would soon reign over the whole world. Each one of us had to buy a book called *The Divine Principles* which we were instructed to read thoroughly while praying to Sun Myung Moon to enlighten us. I tried to decline the book, mainly owing to its expense, but they became extremely insistent and it became clear I wasn't going to leave until I had bought it. Therefore, with book in hand, I left.

The weekend over, I resolved that because I had been so greatly disturbed by it all I would have no more to do with it. That was it –

finished! Oh that it had been, but it wasn't that easy. They relentlessly contacted me until I went for another weekend. This was worse by far than the first, because this was geared to people who had already been before and now the mealtimes and meetings were seriously intense and directly personal to each one of us. I was told that several specific things about me indicated that the spirit world was all around me and was revealing divine truth to me and that I was being called to serve the Great Master, Sun Myung Moon. My destiny and future were no longer in my hands. The spirits of my ancestors were speaking to me and drawing me, and I had to follow. At one mealtime, a German woman, one of the leaders, described in shocking terms the terrible judgements that befell those who failed to respond and give up all to follow the Master. Specific curses were outlined – firstly, you would lose something that belonged to you and it would be the first signal, then you would lose something of great value, and it would be the second signal. If you still failed to respond you would have an accident, fourthly a serious accident, and if you still turned your back on following Sun Myung Moon, then someone in your family would die and you would know for certain that you were severely disobeying the almighty father by failing to follow Sun Myung Moon. As dreadful as this was, the worst was the terrifying description of the horrors of hell that awaited you. The whole weekend was truly frightening.

After a long journey home on the Sunday night, I had to go to work in those beautiful offices the next day with the amiable people I worked with. But all was different. Nothing was beautiful anymore. I was scared and frightened and could talk to no one, friend or family. Whoever would understand? I am glad that, looking back, I made a decision, that although I believed in Sun Myung Moon (and I truly did) I would not go. I simply could not walk out of my family's life and cause such disruption. I knew no more joy and could barely converse with people, but somehow I would have to try and forget this most awful experience.

What a hope! What a hope in hell! There is no hope in hell and that was where I had been led to. Sleepless nights, voices, nightmares, mental images. Still I hung onto my decision. One night as I lay scared in bed, I heard a voice over my head say, "Sun Myung Moon is Lord," and a ball of light hovered over my head and changed into a ball of fire, this fire seemed to come inside me and my whole body raged in a burning heat. I knew nothing then of "demons" or evil spiritual forces, for I had never read the Bible. I had never even owned one. If I had, I might have read that Jesus Christ on this earth encountered such powers many times and delivered people from their evil power.

And then came THE phone call. I was in my office at work typing a long and difficult assignment. The phone rang and it was the German lady. "When are you coming?"

I was stunned it was her. I chose to be evasive. "I don't know, I'm still thinking about it."

"You have no choice; you have to come."

"I can't come. I cannot leave my job here and I cannot just leave my family like this."

"You have been chosen and called; you must come by tomorrow. You have left it too long already. Father is displeased."

"I feel very uneasy about this. I cannot just go like this."

"The whole spirit world is calling you, even your own ancestors. You have no alternative. There are curses that will come upon you and your family."

"I have to give a month's notice here and there is no way I could possibly travel here from Reading."

"Do you love God?"

"Yes."

"God will find a way. You are to be here by tomorrow." CLICK

I was totally devastated. It was the very last phone call I wanted to receive. But now – I had to obey. I had no choice, no alternative. The fact that I felt that I had no alternative may seem incredible to the reader, but looking back I believe that at this time sinister powers were at work in my life, leading me in an ever downward spiral.

My family were devastated when I told them in a simple and matter of fact way that I was leaving the next day. With shaking hands, I packed my new case and in a restless night feared the awful unknown I was walking into. One leader of the group had told me that I was never to see my family again because they were as Satan. Everything to do with my old life was satanic, even my mind was satanic, and I was not to listen to my mind.

The First Day

I left home the next morning and took one backward glance. My life would never be the same again. It was a miserable journey. I sat next to my usual travelling companion on the work's bus that wove its way all around the small outlying Berkshire villages, a bright young lady, Beverley, who showed some concern over the little I told her. "However," she concluded, "if you sincerely believe in what you are doing, then it must be right." It was the only comfort I received that day, but I was later to learn that believing sincerely in something means nothing; you can be sincerely wrong!

I managed to work through my day and that evening, from work, walked to a railway station and caught a train to Reading and a bus to Dunsden and from there walked a good mile through remote countryside to Rowlane Farm. By the time I got there it was already dark. I was utterly miserable, but at least I thought they'll be pleased to see me. They'll be so glad to know that I've joined them to serve in their dedicated mission to usher in the world rule of Sun Myung Moon.

When I arrived, the German leader, who was usually only seen at meals, had not told anyone that I was coming, or of her pressurised phone call to me, insisting that I came that day. The Family members who were there seemed totally surprised to see me and received me coldly.

"What are you doing here? What do you want?"

"I've come to join you, to join the Unification Family and to serve Father."

"Wait outside until the leaders have been informed."

In a while the morose and tired-looking young man returned.

"You are too satanic to come inside, and you are wearing worldly clothes. You must come into the barn outside."

I was led into a dark barn where a dim light showed a mountain of ragged clothes. "These clothes are left over from the jumble sales we hold, but they have been dedicated to Father. Your clothes must be got rid of and you must change into some of these. All the clothes you have brought in your case must be got rid of or burnt or they will contaminate us. Open your case and let me see what else you have brought. I opened my case and he looked sullenly at the simplest of items I had brought. "Most of this is satanic, I will have to get rid of them." This cold reception was a great shock and I pointed out some essential items I thought I would need to keep. He reluctantly condescended and agreed that some could stay out here in the barn, and some could be consecrated. Looking most displeased, he bundled up most of my things and left while telling me to be changed into some of the jumble by the time he returned. I changed and also selected a couple of extra changes of clothes.

When he returned, he brought with him a packet of salt. "Because you have come from the outside world and are satanic you are to be purified with this salt. He then took some salt and, scattering it over me, prayed a prayer to Sun Myung Moon, consecrating me and my last few possessions to him. At last we headed for the farm.

As I entered, no one spoke. Indeed, people seemed to turn and walk away. I assumed that they thought I might contaminate them. Tersely, the young man told me to follow him and led me through a myriad of hitherto unseen corridors and narrow, winding stairs until we came to a top attic. It appeared to be an empty bare room with bare floorboards, two chests of drawers and one small wardrobe. In a corner lay a pile of thin plastic mattresses (palliasses) and some blankets.

"What is this room used for?" I asked.

"This is the girls' bedroom."

"Where are the beds?"

"Nobody sleeps on a bed here. You sleep on the floor; it is all to pay off your sin to Holy Father. You must understand that you are steeped in sin and Satan's world and that you must work off your sins through sufferings called conditions and through the leaders' chastising you. It's called the Law of Indemnity. We owe this to Father. He has loved us so much; we must give our all to him. Your whole life is one of total dedication to him now and you must learn to serve without ever questioning. Your very mind is satanic, so you must not listen to it, you must not answer anyone back. This is how you make restitution. Everyone here is more advanced than you. Some people here have been serving Master for years."

"Where shall I put my clothes I have brought in?" I asked. He went to the chest of drawers and opened a top tiny drawer of about 6 inches wide. He took everything that was in that drawer and pushed it into another drawer.

"Use that," he said, "and if you have any clothes to hang put them in the wardrobe."

I opened it and it was already full. "Does everyone share this one wardrobe?" I asked.

"Nobody owns anything here. Anything hung in there belongs to everyone. You wear anything that is in there each day."

All of this was so startlingly unexpected to me. Nothing of this had been mentioned during the weekends I had been there. I was really beginning to be frightened by the gravity of what I was entering into, and the severity of the attitude shown to me.

"Does nobody own anything here?"

"This is another way in which we pay off our sin to Father. To own something means that you are putting it before God. To say something is 'mine' reveals selfishness and sin and makes Father weep, for it shows how steeped in sin we still are. The disciples in the Acts of the Apostles had all things in common and that is how we live here."

I emptied out my new case of its few contents and he took the case down into the basement. He said it would come in useful for the leaders' travels.

I followed him down and he said that everybody worked until 4 am each morning and there would be a simple supper at a set time which was done by those on kitchen duty. I was only to speak if it was strictly necessary because speaking was of this world. Father was only interested in the spirit, and if we were truly in harmony with him, the spirit world and one another, we would know each other's thoughts.

I was worried about this aspect because I so wanted to be able to obey, but if I could not read the others' minds, what was I to do? He told me that when you speak something, you earth that idea and it becomes of this world, even satanic. To keep ideas pure and spiritual you must keep them in the mind alone. I didn't dare mention that he'd previously said that the mind itself was satanic. As I thought it through, I came to the conclusion that the spirit was above the mind and that was the only realm we were to operate on. How did it work out in practice? At the end of the day, although the conditions appeared harsh to a new girl like me, I truly wanted to serve Divine Master and nobody had forced me to come here! I wanted to make the best of it.

I was put to work in silence scrubbing the floor in a large empty hallway. I worked till I was exhausted. I was later called to a small supper where the one of the senior leaders, Debbie* presided. She seemed genuinely pleased to see me and was greatly gratified. "You have pleased the Father's heart," she said. She seemed all fun and laughter, but she was the only one who was allowed to be. I later learned that this was because she had already worked her way through many conditions and had reached a state of perfection. She and her husband John had been married in divine marriage and had a two-year-old child who lived there too, though I never saw her.

After supper I cleaned the bathrooms and then the floors. Whenever I saw anyone else, they were simply working hard at polishing a table or cleaning silverware and looked neither to the left nor the right. I was quickly learning that constant work purified us and helped to subjugate the body and pay off our great debt of sin. At 4 am everyone seemed to disappear. I was exhausted, so made my way back to the attic where the girls, all aged in their late teens and early twenties, were silently taking a palliasse and a blanket, finding a space on the floor and lying down. Within two minutes the light was out and it was pitch black. Good job I came up when I did.

---

* Not her real name.

18

I was desperately tired and wanted to sleep, but my mind feared greatly. What an end to a most awful and ghastly day. And the worst was that it was only just beginning…

An Even Worse Day

The next morning, I was awoken by a single kick and the words, "Get up." I rose immediately and stacked my palliasse and blanket. No one spoke. I took my washing items and went to the bathroom on the next landing. I discovered about half a dozen girls all using the bathroom at the same time in virtual silence. One was having a cold bath while several were queuing up to use the bath immediately after, another was washing her hair in cold water, another washing her face and another using the loo. Everyone was very austere.

I usually dressed smartly as a secretary and did my hair and put on make-up. Today I was aware how shabby I looked. I got out some brushes and make-up, after all everyone was completely ignoring me. Then the harsh voice of a leader spoke. "You have no need of that. No one here wears make-up – it is all giving attention to self. It is not honouring to Father." I put it away and went downstairs. Those on kitchen duty had made a huge saucepan of porridge. I was so grateful and gulped down a bowlful and left quickly for work – I had a long new walk across fields in the early dawn and no idea what time the buses ran in the next village. I was dreadfully tired and only an unhappy adrenalin drove me on. I must serve Father.

Eventually I was on a bus and then a train. How would I ever stay awake? What did I look like? Whatever would my work colleagues think? At last I arrived at Culham and actually got through a day's work. I was in turmoil, but outwardly I made out that I was very happy. Everyone was aware that something strange was happening and they were embarrassed at my clothes. It was the mini skirt era and I was now wearing an old shapeless skirt well below my knees. During that day I wrote out my notice and handed it in. How upset my parents would be if they knew, but then they would never know; they belonged to a past I could never return to.

That evening I returned again to Rowlane Farm. This time my presence was completely taken for granted. I felt like dropping but no words of greeting were exchanged. It would have been too earthly. It would have brought the world in. A leader approached and told me to go to an upstairs room to clean the floor. He reminded me to constantly subjugate Satan as he is always rising up in our old nature.

After about 20 minutes he came up to the room where I was cleaning and said, "Do you have any bank accounts or building society accounts?"

I told him that I had only a bank account. "How much do you have in it?"

I told him.

"Can you get to your bank in your lunch time?" "Yes." I was unprepared for the next statement.

"Right, well, go in tomorrow and draw out all of it and bring it all into the office downstairs when you come in tomorrow evening. We need money for Father's mission. Do you understand?"

"Yes."

His visit had been less than 5 minutes. He had simply come in and asked me for everything I had and then left. I was never asked to go to that particular isolated room again, and it occurred to me a long time after that the sole reason I was sent to clean it was so that I could be approached and questioned entirely alone.

At the time, although I was taken aback, I thought, "I must do this for Father. This will pay off a great deal of my sins and make me more worthy in Father's eyes. I must give cheerfully for if I have reluctance, Father will know and will be displeased with my gift."

I continued to clean the room thoroughly and later another Family member came and told me that tonight, and every Tuesday, instead of going to "bed" at 4 am, we would go at 1 am, then get up at 3 am by candlelight in absolute silence, wash our hair in cold water and put on totally clean clothes and purify ourselves with salt. Then we would descend downstairs (the boys ascend from the basement) and all gather in the main lounge. There we would say The Divine Pledge to Holy Master.

It all happened as I was told. When we reached the lounge, that too, was in darkness lit only by candles. Standing upright was a gigantic photograph of Sun Myung Moon and nearby a smaller photograph of Holy Mother. Everyone was extremely serious and then fell on their knees, bowing down before the great images and began to worship.

I knew very little of the Bible, yet somewhere, in my very tired, bewildered mind, an alarm bell rang. Didn't one of the Ten Commandments forbid this very thing? There can be only one true God and why would He condemn this and yet here command that we do it? I remembered learning about Daniel, who was thrown to a lion's den because he refused to bend the knee to an image. I was far too terrified in that electrifying atmosphere to openly refuse. I had an uncanny feeling of being in a lion's den. Somehow I managed to cower in a shadowy corner.

Then we all had to stand solemnly upright and recite The Pledge which was a document handed to us. It was a long fervent statement in which we pledged ourselves, time, service and goods to Divine Master for the rest of our lives.

After this we turned and without a word returned to our floorboards to sleep another two hours before the kicking awake and another day.

It sounds crazy, but after weeks of virtually no sleep I used to long for Tuesday nights, because it added up to four hours sleep, an untold luxury. I learned that at 3 am the spiritual air waves were clear and that was why we rose at such an "unearthly" hour!

How many more unearthly things was I going to have to endure to satisfy Father, the Great Master? Where was it all going to end?

Satan's A Hard Task Master

Weeks, months, passed. I was a zombie, a sort of spiritual robot. I no longer thought or reasoned, I just constantly prayed to Father and awaited instructions and obeyed. Father wept over me because I had so much sin; I had so much restitution to make. The Law of Indemnity pushed me to my uttermost limits of doing all that I could to reduce that debt, and even the debt of my ancestors who were depending on me in the spirit world. They were constantly around me, imploring me to serve Sun Myung Moon harder and harder. I fasted three or four days weekly, which was a total food fast and ate almost nothing but rice in the days between. As well as the required morning ice-cold bath, I set myself other conditions. I caused myself pain and hardships and slavishly endured the bitter lashings of the leaders' tongues as they chastised me for my spiritual good. I walked the streets for hours talking to endless people and inviting them to come for weekends. This was called witnessing. I had to follow them up later with letters written on my knees on the floorboards in the bare attic.

Physically I was ill and weak, but I kept walking around and wearing a smile on my face that was far from real. I had not had a menstrual cycle for months and once broke my silence to mention this to an older member. She replied abruptly, "No one here has periods. They stop soon after you come." Much later it occurred to me that that was a sign of just how malnourished every girl was and what strain we lived under.

I had worked out my notice at Culham Laboratories long ago. What sadness to leave a place where I had been so very happy, but as my leaders had told me, I had no alternative but to leave once the divine truth had been revealed to me. I had to obey Master no matter what it cost. Shortly before I left, a new girl joined Culham called Jackie. She heard of my involvement with Sun Myung Moon and asked to sit with me one lunch break. She was friendly and kind but spoke directly and clearly.

"Does this man say that he is the Messiah?"

I was evasive, because we were forbidden to tell anyone that he did. Only Family Leaders could reveal this to chosen and prepared people. However, she noticed that I did not deny it.

"Did you know that Jesus Christ gave very strong and clear warnings about anyone who claims to be the Messiah? He said that many would come in His Name saying, 'I am He,' but do not believe any of them. For as the lightning shines from the east to the west so shall the return of the Son of man (the Messiah) be."

Actually, I knew none of this and should have listened closer, but already I was deeply indoctrinated in my faith and so felt that I had a superior knowledge. Jackie said everything she could to warn me, but I just didn't have the spiritual perception to understand.

I was really like the poor blind beggar in the Bible story, struggling up the hot and dusty road to Jericho where thieves frequently lay in wait. If only, like that beggar, I had reached out to the one who, through Jackie's gentle Christian witness, passed by me that day.

But as He passed by, I turned and walked away. The moment had gone.

I hadn't listened, but I shall always be grateful to Jackie, because she tried to reach me, and I know she also started to pray for me.

I thought that once I had finished at Culham, the Unified Family would want me to work all day in the farmhouse cooking and cleaning and going out witnessing, but I was told that I must immediately get another job in Reading because I must earn money for Father. Courage's Brewery took me on as Secretary to the Brewing Manager, Mr. Mathews. It was in a deep basement office with one high little barred window, next to huge sacks of hops. Mice abounded, and in the mornings I would have to shake the mice droppings off my typing paper. It was a far cry from Culham but I was earning money and one of the Family Leaders lost no time in telling me that I must give their bank account number so that all monies were paid directly to them. Once again I obeyed like a robot. If I thought any differently Father would read my mind and be displeased.

You may wonder how I ever kept a job down. I was driven by a relentless inner power that would drive me until I collapsed. I was like someone who no longer thought but merely awaited instructions. I would take the shorthand notes down from my boss's dictation, go to the typewriter, type-up the letters and lay them on his desk. No conversation, no emotion, and by this time very rarely a coffee or lunch as I was simply given no money. I was only allowed the exact fare for my bus. After the lunch break I would be asleep over my typewriter.

No one would wake me up for they all knew that I got very little sleep, except, of course, Mr. Mathews, who would lightly shake me and ask if I was ready for some more dictation. Very fortunately he was a good-humoured man who took it all in his stride! I would wake up and carry on like a machine. I never laughed; I had totally forgotten what laughter or happiness was. But that was good because that proved to Master that I was dedicated and helped to pay sin off.

I thought that if I continued in this way for 12 years, it may be that I would work myself to a degree of perfection whereby I could be married in one of Mr. Moon's mass wedding ceremonies when Mr. Moon would select a foreign partner on the day. We would not be able to live together, but at a certain stage, when we had gained sufficient credit, we would be allowed to have a child. This child would be perfect and an inheritor of the Kingdom of God. We had no hope of the kingdom ourselves but paved the way for our children. Already there were some 200 of these children in the world. The natural parents were not allowed to raise these children. After all their years of suffering conditions and restitution they might possibly be able to glimpse the kingdom of heaven from afar. Looking back now, I wonder whoever thought up this doctrine?

Holy Father's Visit

One evening at a mealtime (we all sat round even if we were fasting), one of our leaders brought us tidings of good news which was to be of great joy to us all. Master was coming to stay two weeks with us! Next week!

We were allowed very little speech but the looks on everyone's faces ranged from sheer disbelief to awesome wonder. The magnitude of it all was too great. I thought he was in Korea, or had I heard a faint rumour that he had been banned from there? Ah, but hadn't Jesus been rejected by his own people?

Poor Jesus, he had tried, but everywhere he went the people rejected him, until finally he was strung up on a cross, abandoned by the very people he came to save. He was a saviour who couldn't save. Even the thief had said, "Save yourself," and he couldn't. The fact that God raised him to life afterwards meant nothing – it was simply God's way of taking him back to heaven after his mission on earth had failed. Satan had jumped on this and made a religion out of it! And people believed it! In fact when you boiled it down, Christians were not merely deluded by Satan but were satanic themselves because they believed Satan's lie. We had been warned a great deal about this prior to witnessing trips. "Christians are the most satanic of all people. Never attempt witnessing to them, and if you discover the person you are with is a Christian, then leave as quickly as possible. Say, 'I am a Christian too,' because Sun Myung Moon is the Christ.'"

That night I lay trembling on my thin palliasse. Sun Myung Moon was the almighty god, maker of heaven and earth; what would it be like to live in the same house as him?

I was to discover a week later.

The moment had arrived. We had cleaned the house as it had never been cleaned before. We had all had cold baths and hair washes. The boys had marched around the frozen ploughed fields with bare feet at unearthly hours to make restitution. We had dressed ourselves in the best of the washed jumble. We stood in silence, just waiting, ready to greet him and bow our heads. Perhaps he would smile on us. Oh, that he would just glance our way.

Suddenly it was happening. From the window we saw a whole fleet of black limousine cars draw up. I have twice seen the Queen arrive at certain venues but never had I seen a cavalcade such as this. There were about seven limousines all packed and chauffeur driven. We straightened ourselves. Suddenly a man ran from a car and spoke rapidly to one of our leaders. The leader ran inside and spoke quickly to us all. "You are all too satanic to be seen. Get out of sight. Go to the attic and basement and do not allow yourselves to be seen by Master – he cannot be contaminated. Now go!" We ran.

None of us spoke so I had no idea what anyone else thought but it was a very great put-down for us all. We had been preparing ourselves for the past week for this with incredible conditions. Possibly Master was displeased with us. We must examine ourselves. Later, one of our leaders, Debbie, came up to our attic, the first time I had ever seen her in there. She was very serious and reaffirmed that none of us at any time must be seen by Master. If by any chance we happened to discover ourselves in his presence we were to totally prostrate ourselves on the ground before him three times and leave. He had brought many servants with him and we were to keep completely separate from them too. Holy Mother of the Earth had also come with him and must be treated likewise.

We sat up there in silence until we slept and then early next morning I left for work. I was in fact glad to get out of the house.

In our many intensive prayer meetings, Debbie had often cried when she described the broken humility of Sun Myung Moon. He carried the compassion of the Father's heart and he loved deeper than words could say. He was the Christ returned and had all power, yet he knew sorrow to the uttermost depths. It was right that I should not see Mr. Moon. I was worth nothing. How would I ever cope with being in the presence of such love and compassion? I hoped desperately I wouldn't meet him by accident.

That evening I went straight to the attic room and stayed there. I was all alone for once. I listened: somewhere far away I could hear shouting. Loud angry shouting. I had often heard shouting before when leaders were chastising younger members. It was always frightening to hear. I tried to ignore it, thinking pure thoughts, but it went on. At last I decided to do the unthinkable – to venture out and discover the source of the shouting. I wove through corridors and followed the sound to the kitchen. I stood outside. No one else was in sight. A man was yelling in a foreign language. Who would dare do this while Master dwelt in the house? Suddenly the tirade stopped and a door angrily slammed. With all my courage I slowly opened the door and stepped inside.

There in a terribly broken state was an older Korean lady. She saw me and fell into my arms. I sat on a chair and held her. I could feel great convulsions of sobs racking her thin body. She was as limp as a rag doll. I stroked her hair and wet, tear-stained face. "What has happened?" I whispered. All she could gasp was, "Master angry. Master angry." I could not believe it – had it been Sun Myung Moon himself who was shouting like that?

"Why was Master angry?"

"He no like food. Food not good."

We had been told that Mr. Moon always travelled with his own cook because she cooked everything especially for him, to exact specifications and to the traditional Korean style. Every cooking item, crockery and cutlery had to be set apart for him and for this reason none of us could enter the kitchen whilst he was there. This lady was a specialized cook and had been preparing food for him all day, and yet this was her reward.

Somewhere in my mind an alarm bell was ringing. This was not how I imagined my god to be, losing his temper like any mere man! I was so glad that I had traced the shouting and gone into the forbidden kitchen because I was able to comfort that dear lady. However, she was all fearful nerves that he would return, and though she could hardly speak English, I gained the impression that she would have to start cooking all over again. With a heavy heart I left her and returned to my attic and to my personal, miserable bewilderment.

Soon after, the others returned from a major witnessing trip. They had communicated to hundreds the good news of the coming Messiah, and their faces were aglow. The world was being prepared. I kept my experience of that evening to myself.

A new message was soon passed around us. Master had said that he would address us that night in the main lounge at 3 am, when the spiritual air was clear. We were stunned. We had given up all hope of seeing him; we were too satanic. Master must be pleased with us to show such grace and mercy.

All the usual preparations were done. The hour came and we solemnly filed down. We were given a final severe warning that we were still satanic, and he was utter purity, so we were to cringe our way into the corners and make ourselves as inconspicuous as possible. This was accepted as normal.

One of our number was a badly crippled young man, whose paralysed leg dragged behind him, yet he drove himself as hard as all the rest of us. I wondered if Mr. Moon would look with compassion and heal him. We had been told that he performed miracles.

We cringed in, about 50 of us, slightly bowing all the time. For a long time, we dared not raise our eyes. When we did lift our eyes, we would behold the most manifold excellence. When I lifted my eyes, I beheld a stern-faced, rotund, oriental, businesslike man. He never looked at any of us but fixed his eyes on the ceiling over and above our heads.

There was hushed silence, then Sun Myung Moon began. He shouted at the top of his voice – in Korean. None of us could understand a word. It was a fact that I don't think had occurred to any of us – that Mr. Moon did not speak a word of English. Beside him stood a very nervous, slim, Korean interpreter. As soon as Mr. Moon would pause for breath he would hurriedly begin to interpret, but within seconds Mr. Moon would start again. This was no ordinary shouting; it was more like hysterical screaming. I began to be clearly reminded of old films I had seen of Hitler screaming in his speeches. Yet for all this volume, very little message, if any, was coming across to us. The only gist I caught at one stage was that God was like an orange. You peeled it and inside were all the segments – so it is with God. Also, he is like a hand – there were all the fingers. He never, however, explained what the segments or fingers stood for. Or perhaps he did and we couldn't hear. The poor interpreter looked worn to a shred and Mr. Moon carried on this incredible speech for three hours. It simply went on and on. All of us existed on very little food and sleep and it was a feat of feats to continue to look attentive. Finally, at 6 am he stopped, and with a dismissal, left the room. Just in time. We were to be starting our day. Without a word we cringed out, the lame boy, still lame, leading the way, and we went to our work.

So this was Sun Myung Moon, the great and terrible one, the almighty one. What shock, what horror! My initial belief in him was more shaken than ever. Alarm bells were ringing in my mind, but what could I do? I had pledged my whole life to this man and given everything I possessed. There was no turning back. How I went and did a day's work I don't know. I felt confused to the point where I simply couldn't think straight.

I returned to Rowlane Farm to be told that Mr. Moon would address us again tonight, this time at 2 am onwards. I don't remember anyone looking glad this time, and the law of silence was very easy to keep now; no one wanted to speak. We were given special permission to sleep at midnight. Unheard of! Sun Myung Moon addressed us every night, all night, for the whole two weeks he was with us; but the more he spoke, the more I began to question the faith I had until then embraced.

Holy Mother Of The Earth

One Saturday, while Father was still with us, a major hall in London was booked and Sun Myung Moon was going to speak publicly! This was to be the first time he was revealed to England! Debbie came to see me and told me that I was to be Holy Mother of the Earth's handmaiden and was to accompany her at all times whilst travelling to and from London and to stay with her throughout the crusade. What an unexpected honour! Me! All my conditions must have stood me in some credit.

The day dawned. I prepared myself and went to her room to meet her. To my utter surprise I met a younger version of the Korean cook. She ran to me and fell into my arms whimpering and shaking. She was evidently underweight. I held her in my arms and tried to comfort her but I quickly realised that she could neither speak nor understand a word of English. I helped her downstairs to a waiting taxi. That entire journey to London she clung to me, weeping. Occasionally she glanced at me but try as she might she could tell me nothing about what was wrong. I felt most perplexed while I held her trembling body.

All I knew about her was that Sun Myung Moon had seen her once amongst his Korean followers and declared that she was chosen to be his wife and to rule with him when his kingdom came. She was worthy of worship – the uttermost honour. She was the mother of his seven children, all of whom were perfect.

When we finally arrived, I wondered how we would ever emerge with dignity and enter the prestigious building, as the Holy Mother seemed totally unable to stand. As I helped her into the large entrance, another servant hurried forward, bowing, and we were quickly hustled into a drab, cold, bare brick waiting room with a few of the other servants. I thought one of them might be able to help and speak to Holy Mother but they all seemed not to notice and to ignore her. Then I realised what was happening – it was unthinkable for any of them to approach her or appear to notice her state – she was far too holy! They dare not even look. No one spoke a word of English so I could not communicate my concerns for her health. We sat there for about an hour. No tea or refreshment was brought to Holy Mother. I supposed we were all fasting. We generally did all the time anyway. By Mr. Moon's size I would think he was the only one who didn't. But of course, he wouldn't need to, he was Divine Master.

At last the order was given and Holy Mother and I were to enter after Master and take our seats in the front row (thank goodness, not on the platform!). As we stood, Holy Mother began to shake again; she really couldn't stand, and I supported her to the utmost of my ability. She was burying her head in my chest and clinging to my clothes. No one came to our aid; no one looked. Instead all the servants stood to rigid attention, some went before us and some behind us. That would at least shield us a little. How we entered I don't know, but enter we did. Holy Mother used supreme effort and for the vital moments we were on display, clinging nervously to my hand, she managed to totter to her seat. All eyes were on Master Moon.

He stood there like a great god, master of heaven and earth. The hall was packed with hundreds! Now he would be recognised for who he was. For the first time in my hearing he did not shout, but it was still all in Korean and there was little understandable in the message despite the interpreter.

All the while Holy Mother was obviously in deep distress and throughout never raised her eyes to look at her divine husband. Instead she continued to cling to me, and I continued to support her body as upright as I could. Oh, that I could have just allowed her to lay her head on my lap and weep. The packed auditorium was whittled down to a shred of about fifty people by the time Sun Myung Moon stopped speaking – about the number of his dedicated followers. Vast sections of the audience had simply walked out at intervals. Moon appeared not to notice – he was looking at the ceiling.

The journey home with Holy Mother was identical to the trip out. Both journeys were the most agonising trips I have ever made. I could not find out what was wrong with Holy Mother that day – all I could do was stroke her trembling head on my lap.

I was fighting sleep. All the questions I had begun to ask myself now pressed me stronger than ever. Had we really found the truth or not?

Or were we somehow all being blinded to it? The question hung in the air, without answer.

Finally, back at Rowlane, Holy Mother was taken to her room by a nervous Korean servant. One of my saddest memories is of seeing her being taken to her room without being able to help. Within a few days she was whisked off to another country.

On another day a leader had asked me to take a glass of milk up to Sun Myung Moon's bedroom. What a surprise. I nervously took it along, praying in His name all along. I went into unknown quarters (how big was this farmhouse?), stepped into his room and discovered myself in another world! I thought I'd found myself in Ali Baba's cave. Numbers of rich tapestries and leopard and tiger skins covered the walls, bed and floor. Rich apparel lay everywhere and costly eastern bowls and ornaments adorned every surface. I stood for a moment and then laid the milk down and returned to the Spartan bareness of our attic room.

He left without having spoken personally or even looked at any of us. He was remote. I personally felt that I had never encountered such a mountain of hardness and pride, but how could I tell? I must make restitution for even thinking it.

A Church With An Open Door

Apart from the week with Mr. Moon, all those weary months are one blur in my memory but I distinctly remember walking down Friar Street in Reading and wishing I was dead. I was thinking through how I could kill myself when another thought struck me. "If I am going to die, and am so confused, then why don't I at least first go into a church, cast myself on the altar and beg God to help me? Perhaps He will do some sort of miracle for me?" I didn't actually know who God was. Was Sun Myung Moon really Jesus Christ?

In my lunch times I went from church to church to discover every door locked. I was quite desperate now because I felt that this was my only hope. One day I walked to one last church, St. Lawrence's near Friar Street – it was open! I stepped into the cold darkness and sat on a back pew, knelt and poured out my troubled soul to a God I didn't know.

I heard a tinkling sound. Oh no. I was not alone. The church was so large and dim I could not see, but I walked slowly down the aisle and discovered a side chapel where a minister was about to serve Holy Communion to three people kneeling at the altar. I couldn't think what they were doing there and it was exactly where I longed to kneel. The minister stopped in his service and looked at me. I looked at him and then because I had to do something, I went and joined the three people at the altar. He came straight to me and gave me some bread. "This represents the body of our Lord Jesus Christ, broken for you. Take and eat." I ate it! What was I doing! He came to me with a cup of wine. "This represents the blood of our Lord Jesus Christ whose blood was shed for you. Take, drink." I drank! Was I allowed to do this? I had denounced all this. I didn't believe in this. This crucified Jesus could not help me – or could he?

The service finished. The people departed. I waited for a long time until I was sure I was alone and then I lay on the altar steps and wept. I desperately wanted to pray but I didn't know how or who to pray to. I found myself, strangely, crying over and over again, "Jesus, save me." They were the only words that came to me and I hadn't a clue why I should say them.

So agonised was my cry that I felt certain God would send an angel, or a vision or speak to me, but … nothing. I waited. Nothing but an empty blank. Now I really knew. There simply was no God. I very slowly walked out and made my way back to Courage's Brewery. I could not have guessed that the true Almighty God had actually listened to every word I had prayed and would answer quickly in a most amazing and unusual way. For now, praying to God seemed pointless.

And who would also have guessed that a member of the Unification Church had secretly followed me into St. Lawrence's Church and had stood in the shadows watching and listening all that time, and would hurry back to report me?

When I got back to Rowlane Farm I was deep in private thoughts. I had just proved that there was no God, yet I had given up everything in his service. I was disillusioned to the point where I was seriously entertaining suicide.

Someone sent me into the kitchen and a very cold reception met me by one of the particularly sour leaders. He rebuked me severely. "You have betrayed Master!"

I couldn't believe what I was hearing. Surely, nobody knew what I had done?

"You have received Holy Communion! You were seen receiving the body and blood of Jesus Christ! Didn't you know that this is the most satanic of all services? That is the worst of the worst. You are not fit to set foot in here. Idiot! Dog! Scum! Don't look so amazed – you were followed. You have utterly degraded all of us spiritually." It carried on and on, far longer than I care to recall here. Once it was finished, I fled to the attic to ponder and think with my befuddled mind. I began to think there were strange forces at loose in this farmhouse, who hated anything to do with Jesus Christ. Why did the very name of Jesus generate such formidable hatred here?

Conflicts Without And Fears Within

The next day I was at work and, as usual now, had not a penny for any lunch so used the time to fast and witness. I went outside Marks & Spencers and witnessed down an entire long bus queue. I was barely coherent. I barely knew who I was or what I was saying. One young man was leaning up against one of the pillars. I went to him and said, "Do you want to have new life in God?" (As if I could offer anyone any guidance.)

He stood upright and smiled at me. "I already have new life in God – through Jesus Christ."

The power with which those words hit me I can barely describe. He had spoken quietly yet it was as if something struck out and hit me. I felt myself reeling and almost passing out. I steadied myself by the pillar and was rendered completely speechless. Everything within me reacted violently to his words. I was aware that this young man possessed a great spiritual power, while I, and indeed all those in The Family, possessed nothing in comparison to this.

He observed my notebook and pen and said, "Shall I write down the name of the house-church where I worship and the couple who run it?"

We were commanded to get names and addresses, so I handed him the book.

I looked at it. John and Marian Shaw and their address and phone number with his own name, Peter Davies.

"What do you do there?" I ventured.

"We just worship the Lord."

I was dumb.

Just then his bus drew in and he bade me farewell with a smile. "Visit John and Marian, they can talk to you further," and with that he was gone.

I was left alone. What had happened? He had said that he already had new life in God through Jesus Christ and at the same time a power flowing from him seemed to strike me, and the opposing forces within me reeled as if from a mighty blow.

All this I mulled over in my 2 hours of troubled sleep and I made the secret decision to phone and visit this John and Marian Shaw immediately after work, and quickly, before I was missed. I was already in the leaders' bad books.

A strange thing happened with this phone call and I felt in the end a sense that a different presence was with me. Some unseen power was helping and guiding me. I could not use the phone at work for a personal call and I only had the exact pence necessary for a public call box (which was a miracle to begin with). I went to an open phone booth and laid the pence by the receiver. Some young men jostled about me, playing around. I searched for my notebook and the telephone number I found it, dialled, turned for my money and it was gone! One of those young men had taken it. I just couldn't believe it. It really was all I had, and with my suicidal thoughts this phone call was life and death to me. It was that important.

I stood completely at a loss. Now all was gone. Then a strange thought struck me. "Go back to your office and the cleaners will let you in. Search through your office drawer and you may just find the coins you need." I thought it was impossible but it was such an insistent thought that I went and did it and to my amazement, scrabbling at the back, I found the exact coins! Remembering how penniless I was day after day, you will realise the miracle of those coins. I have often wondered if an angel put them there.

I made the phone call. A pleasant voice answered and said, "Come over," and gave me directions. John and Marian Shaw's home was like a foretaste of heaven.

Those quiet, gentle and lovely people opened their home to a weird young lady that evening. John simply said, "Tell us about yourself." Marian brought in a tray of coffee and biscuits and I couldn't believe that I was sitting in an armchair and a drink was being brought to me. I told them at length of my joining the Unification Church and of Mr. Moon. I spoke as a true believer in him, unswerving in devotion. I must not voice any of my recent doubts.

At the end John said, "May I share with you my faith in Jesus Christ?"

"Yes," I stammered realising that in one gentle sweep he was putting the Master aside and bringing Jesus to the fore. John quietly and simply talked about Jesus Christ, His purpose, His ministry and His crucifixion when He died to pay the price of sin, even original sin. His salvation was total and complete. He died according to God's plan and purpose as shown in Isaiah 53, and He gained the greatest victory that mankind has ever known. By rights we should die a sinner's death, but Jesus died it in our place, that those of us who receive Him into our lives may go free before God.

I had a very confused, tired mind. I was still a worshipper of Moon and, just as Jackie had tried to talk to me, I listened but I could neither hear, nor understand. But this I knew. In this home was peace, love, kindness and understanding. Furthermore, while John spoke a beautiful and warm presence filled the room. It was like oil sweeping and washing over me. I basked in it, relaxed in it; it lingered all around me and anointed me. If ever there was a Holy Spirit, He was in this room, washing me, drawing me to Him.

I had never experienced anything like this before. It was totally different to the tense, electrifying atmosphere at the farm. These people were quite obviously worshippers of God. I almost lowered my defences, I almost believed, and then I was aware of another voice, "What you are doing? You are betraying Father! You have been warned about Christians." I stood up. "I must go now, thank you for the coffee." They quickly escorted me to the door. I would leave as quickly as possible. I must not be missed.

I hesitated at the door. The cold blackness of the wintry night faced me, somehow it epitomised my true state. No matter, I must go and face the long walk into the emptiness. "Please let me drive you to wherever you need to get to."

Their kindness knew no bounds. I could hardly believe that these very kind people, that I was rejecting, were not only willing to receive a stranger into their home, but then to drive them to their destination.

I swallowed the pride that would have refused and gratefully accepted. I had to get back as quickly as possible. The Family had an uncanny way of discovering where you had been and if you had done anything to betray Father.

I reached the farm. I hadn't been missed. From that time on, John and Marian and Peter Davies began to pray for me.

A Locked Door

Life in the Moonies carried on doubly hard, for since Father's visit our conditions and witnessing had to be greatly increased.

His kingdom would soon come on this earth and we had to usher it in. Our lives were an endless treadmill of relentless activity to subjugate Satan and make restitution. We never sat down, hardly slept and fasted continually. Endless conditions were set. Frenzied high-powered prayer meetings went on with Debbie able to communicate with many spirits around us. They all testified to Sun Myung Moon as the Great Messiah and urged us to work harder, ever harder.

During this hive of exhausting activity a new forbidden thought came to me. "Go home and see your parents." Impossible! Not allowed! I would be bitterly chastised, perhaps even thrown out. It would damage the spirit world that we were working so hard to restore.

"Go home anyway." Where did this insistent thought come from? It's totally forbidden. Father will be very displeased.

"One of the commandments is to honour your father and your mother." Something or someone was speaking to me. Yes, of course, this was one of the Ten Commandments. How strange that Moon actually forbade one of the commandments. How extraordinary and I had never even thought of it. Yes, I would go, but how? There was only one way, to go in my usual work hours. In fact this Friday was a bank holiday, and I was sure the farm did not know I was due the day off.

And so I went. I was extremely broken up and sad because I had only on the last Tuesday night pledged myself once again to Moon in the 3 am ceremony and I knew that these few hours would be the very last time I would ever see my parents again. I must never make a second visit. Thoughts of suicide were also continually with me.

But things were to take a very different turn.

I hadn't the faintest notion what day it was. As soon as I eventually arrived home, my shocked mother said, "It's Good Friday and Dad is just taking us to the Good Friday service in Blewbury." My heart sank. Oh no! I could not have arrived on a worse day in the whole year.

My parents were Anglicans and every Good Friday we always attended a full three-hour meditation service. My memories were of a long endurance test, but it had been unthinkable not to go. Now it was totally different – it was unthinkable to go.

Dad came in. I believe they were playing down the enormous occasion of my unexpected visit.

"We're just about to go to the Good Friday service, we can all go together."

"I'm not going." All this effort and I was simply going to have to sit at home alone.

"Of course you are coming. We have never missed Good Friday. It's when the Lord died."

"I don't believe any of that. In fact, I have renounced all that. It's actually evil." A hardness came over me. No wonder we were forbidden to come home, if we were going to encounter this sort of thing.

Dad's temper rose up powerfully against me. "What on earth are you saying? Don't you suddenly turn up here and say things that amount to no more than rubbish."

My temper rose up. I won't begin to recall it all, but Dad and I had a major row, flinging words at one another. Eventually, Dad physically pushed me towards the car, Mum opened the door, and he threw me in and slammed the door. He and Mum jumped in and Dad sped off. I was livid. I was totally beside myself with anger. This was outrageous and disastrous!

Dad drove as fast as he could to prevent my leaping out, which of course I was looking for every opportunity to do. We arrived at the very large old parish church of Blewbury. Dad said some extremely firm words to me and he and Mum frogmarched me into that dim, dark, centuries old church. Never did three more angry people enter a church for the Good Friday three-hour meditation service.

I knew I had lost the battle, but I remained incensed. We walked to a pew and my parents sat either side of me. This was unbelievable that I should be forced to come to such a satanic service as this. And for three hours! The restitution I would have to make! There was only one possible hope and that was to inwardly chant, "I subjugate Satan," continuously throughout the whole service, as we were rigourously taught by the Family Leaders.

The service started and droned on. I subjugated Satan all the time. The minister got up and spoke. I never heard a word, I was in my own world. "Oh God why don't you help me? I subjugate Satan. Help me. I subjugate Satan." At last the minister stopped. "And now we shall sing hymn number 587." The organ started. There are some moments that you never forget your whole life long, and I shall never forget the next few moments or what happened next as long as I live. I reached for the hymn book. I thought mockingly, "Hymn number 587. So what? What can a hymn do? Will this hymn change my life?"

The first line started: "Oh Jesus Thou Art Standing Outside the Fast Closed Door."

In that moment Jesus stood right before me about a foot away. It was not an inward vision, He was actually there, full bodily, as real and solid as any human being. It was unmistakably Jesus and at the same time I knew that I was in the presence of the Almighty God. Yet He stood there simply and humbly before me in a plain robe and in His crucified state. He was right there in front of me, yet He never looked at me. His eyes were cast down to the ground. I knew that He could not look at me for there was no fellowship at all between us. If He had looked at me I could never have taken His gaze. His very look would have seared through me and spoken my condemnation without a word. I knew that though in my heart of hearts I had sought Him, I had nothing to do with Him nor He with me. Yet here He was, just standing before me.

The hymn continued. I had never heard this hymn before and yet every line became etched within me and before my eyes the hymn became real.

Jesus' head was covered in a crown of thorns. Bitter, long, callous thorns that were thrust hard down upon His head and crushed deeply into His skin. He bled streams of blood from every thorn so that His face was covered in blood, and still the blood ran. No memory of a picture book told me this was Jesus; He was beyond recognition. No artist ever painted this.

I stood and stared. I, who had denied His crucifixion, was seeing so vividly the extremity of this suffering, and I was aware that in some way it was for me. I became conscious of a massive and heavy door between us, yet I could see clearly through it. The door was like the huge, thick oak door of a castle. I saw every detail, the planks it was made from and how they were laid across, the great studs, the huge round handle, but my attention was arrested by all the locks on the door!

I had never seen so many locks of every kind – and every one was locked. Great keys and drawn bolts rusted solidly into place. There was no hope of ever opening that door. And then even as I looked, I saw that great door was covered with ivy, brambles and thorns growing all over it. That door had been shut fast for many years.

And then I saw even worse. He lifted up His hand and I saw the most wretched sight. It was the most appalling mess you can imagine. It was hardly a hand, yet I knew it was. Great nails had been driven in and they had supported the weight of his body for six hours. The holes gaped, the flesh was ripped, and blood ran profusely. He lifted this hand towards the door, and He began knocking on it. I couldn't think why. The knuckles that did the knocking were devoid of flesh and He knocked on bare bones. I stood mortified and looking.

Time passed into eternity and so did speech. I started to speak to Jesus and He to me, yet no words were said. It was a communication in the spirit.

"Are you bearing the sin of the world?"

"I am bearing your sin."

"Why are knocking on this door?"

"This is the door of your heart."

"What are all these bolts?"

"Every time I knocked, you drew another bolt."

'Why are Your hands like that?"

"This is how long I have been knocking."

I wept. All around people were singing, oblivious. The Prince of Peace stood before me, broken, crucified, knocking and I stood there in pride locking Him out. Who was I, a mere mortal, that I could do this to the Lord of Glory?

I had sought God so much, yet I was locked out. How could I undo those bolts? I continued staring and the whole time He knocked. The hymn drew to its close and I was alone between my parents. Everyone was sitting down as if nothing had happened.

Odd as it may seem I was incapable of rational thought and remained still very uncommunicative.

At home I shut myself in my bedroom and tried to think. What a strange experience. What did it all mean? How could I ever open that door and how had I locked it?

"Oh look at the time! I must go, I must be back by my usual time or the Family Members may find out."

Mum and Dad begged me to stay, but it was out of the question. They could see I was making ready to run the three miles to the train station so, seeing there was no hope, Dad drove me. How heavy his heart must have been.

Rowlane Farm at last. No one would ever guess where I had been. But the moment I entered I was told immediately to report to John, the senior leader who marched me to yet another room I had never seen and unleashed his fury upon me. What could he be so angry about? Surely no one could have found out. To this day I don't know how they found out, but they did and I suffered the dire consequences. John swore the air blue, which surprised me. Wasn't he someone who had reached sinless perfection and was perfectly holy?

I had at last been allowed to return to our dorm, but I was little more than a washed-out dishcloth in a heap on that drab attic floor.

I thought to myself, "Master must be very angry. I must completely re-dedicate my life to him yet again. Please forgive me, Holy Father. I give my life to you."

Afterwards I scrubbed floors till 4 am and at last lay asleep on the floor for the precious 2 hours sleep. But I couldn't sleep.

Jesus was there in my mind. Knocking, knocking, knocking. "Jesus, where are you and who are you? Help me. Save me. All I wanted was to know Your kingdom and now I know that I'm locked outside. Show me what this door is. If only I could unlock it."

And so it continued night after night. I would toss and turn restlessly. It seemed like an immense spiritual battle was waging around me and within me. While I was fully going Master's way, it had seemed easier, but now it seemed that forces of darkness were opposing an enemy with all their strength. That enemy was a penetrating ray of light.

A Confused Mind Becomes Crystal Clear

I managed yet another day's work at Courages and was now back at the farm and cleaning in the kitchen.

"Leave cleaning that sink and get out to the van and go witnessing." I hurried to obey the call.

Soon we were piling out into the cold, dark evening air somewhere in Reading. Everyone was quickly in pairs except me. I was the odd one. The leader looked exasperated. Hadn't we counted correctly?

He looked at a loss and then said, "Go to the library and look up a religious meeting and go and break it up and tell everyone about Messiah. Take this bag full of leaflets and give them out but be sure to be back here for the mini-van."

This was the first time I had ever been sent out alone in an evening and on such a task. In the library I studied the local newspaper. There was an advert for a Gospel Rally, whatever that was. It sounded religious. Well, I'd better go.

Gospel Rally. Underwood Free Church, the "Come Back To God" Campaign, Whitley Estate, Reading. At last I found it and arrived in time for the start. I stared down the pathway to what looked like a plain rather old building. I didn't really want to go in, and especially to break it all up, but I had to.

I slowly started to walk up the pathway. Unbeknown to me, the visiting evangelist, Ben Belsham, was looking out the window and praying about the service that evening. As he saw me, he felt the Holy Spirit all around him and he felt a voice say, "The girl coming up the pathway now has been sent by Me. She is under a satanic delusion and needs deliverance to be set free." Ben Belsham bowed his head and prayed.

I entered. Straight away I was struck by the atmosphere. It was like John and Marian Shaw's home. Peace, happiness and love was in every face and every warm welcome. I stood quietly not daring to absorb it; after all, I had orders to break all this up.

I sat down and my attention was arrested by two large scriptures above the platform. "Jesus Christ, the Same, Yesterday, Today and Forever" and "I know That My Redeemer Lives." It struck me that both scriptures knocked Sun Myung Moon on the head. How strange that I knew no scriptures. I suddenly realised that I had never seen a Bible at Rowlane Farm. It was possibly too dangerous a book.

They sang hymns and choruses I'd never heard. People got up and spoke of Jesus coming into their lives, and being converted and born again, and their lives changed. I had never heard of such things, yet the people spoke with one accord and radiated a glowing joy.

Then Pastor Ben Belsham got up to speak. "The scripture I am going to speak on comes from the Book of Revelation, chapter 3 and verse 20." Everyone got out a Bible and looked it up. I would have to listen.

He read, "Behold I stand at the door and knock. If anyone hears My voice, and opens the door, I will come in and eat with him and he with me."

I sat there in a daze. Was I really hearing right? I had no idea that the manifestation of Jesus that I had so clearly seen was taken right out of the Bible – in fact from Revelation which was a book we at Rowlane Farm were always talking about but didn't actually know anything about.

Pastor Ben enlarged the scripture and spoke at length on the full meaning of the words. "Each one of us is locked out of God's kingdom. We lock ourselves out through our sins and our tendency to listen to the devil. Jesus knocks on that door in many ways and we can turn our backs and walk away. We need to behold Jesus dying on that cross for each one of us personally and to accept His death in our place to pay the price for our salvation. By doing this we open the door to Jesus and we welcome Him into our lives to reign as Lord and Saviour. Jesus can save you this very day."

It was the very message I had been longing to hear! It was the key to the lock!

The service ended and I didn't know what to do. A myriad of inner conflicting voices spoke to me. "You must reject all this. They do not know about Master, Messiah and his kingdom. He is greater still. You must give out his leaflets." I wearily and without heart began to give out the Moon leaflets, my brain in a daze. I had hardly slept the last week and even today I was on a total fast for Master. Pastor Ben was at my side within seconds.

"Welcome! You are a newcomer here. What organisation are you involved with?" I handed him a leaflet and he saw instantly what it was. He then told me of His experience with the Holy Spirit when he had first seen me. The moment he said the words, I knew that it was completely true. I could have wept that God loved me this much.

The resident minister of the church, Pastor Jim Morris, joined us. "Shall we talk to her in the vestry?" he quietly suggested. "No," muttered Pastor Ben, "she's like a wild woman, talking would do no good. She needs prayer."

I stood silently not daring to speak. "May I pray for you?" he asked. I nodded. Pastor Ben put his hand on my head and prayed in a foreign language. I had thought he was English. The strange language continued, and something began to happen. Something quite dynamic. Something lifted off me and harassing voices were quelled. My mind became crystal clear and suddenly I could think! I could think any thought I wished and easily! I could rationalise, reason and understand clearly. Suddenly I understood the truth. I saw clearly the gospel message. That Jesus died for me. FOR ME. I understood totally that Jesus, not Sun Myung Moon, was the true God I was looking for. The great door was creaking, and rust was falling off ancient bolts.

I stood and stared at Pastors Ben and Jim. "I feel set free!"

Someone brought me a cup of tea and the two ministers continued to talk to me about truth and error, the scriptures and what they had to say about the return of Christ. I drank in everything and began to converse and talk fluently for the first time since joining the Family. It was the most incredible miracle that I could think clearly and talk freely again. I could have laughed and cried all night.

But suddenly I realised the time. The minibus – I must be back, what can I do? A kind soul immediately offered to drive me, and I began to grab my things. It strikes me as amazing that I risked going back, but it was my home.

Quickly Pastor Ben said, "If you want to become a Christian; then be back here tomorrow evening on our last night."

My heart sank, "That's almost impossible," I stammered. They didn't know the strict regime of orders given and the instant obedience that was demanded. I could be sent anywhere. "With God nothing is impossible. We will pray for you." I hurriedly ran to my lift and caught the bus back to the farm.

WHAT A DAY!

But what about tomorrow?

Saved

Kick. "Get up." The usual awakening could not deter my happiness. As I arose I realised that I had slept, well and good, for the first time for at least a month. I longed to shout from the rooftops and swing from a chandelier, but I dared not speak. In fact, I tried not to look happy – it would look strange and attract suspicion. I would be reported. That would put an end to everything.

I quickly hurried to make the long early walk across the fields. As I was leaving one of the leaders caught my arm – "Sign this before you go." He held a form in his hand. "Yes, have you got a pen?"

"Haven't you got one?" he sounded irritated. "Look in your bag." I scrabbled through and found a pencil and signed. He was very annoyed. "A pencil signature is no good on an official document like this. They probably won't accept it."

"What is it?" I trembled as we were not allowed to ask questions. I glanced at the form, trying to read the print. "It covenants your salary to us for the next seven years so that we can regain the tax. Go and find a pen."

Praise God I had a clear mind now and an iota of boldness. "I'm sorry, I daren't, I shall miss my bus and be late for work and I may lose my job. They have already been noticing how tired I am."

I was released. God had delivered me from signing that form. Unknown to me, Ben Belsham and Jim Morris were already praying and fasting for my complete deliverance. Can I ever thank God enough for them?

That evening I returned to Rowlane after work. "Oh Lord," I prayed, "they said that with you nothing is impossible, please open up the way for me to get back to Underwood Free Church tonight."

Everyone was extremely busy. I was delighted to notice the minibuses were being got ready for witnessing teams; I was nearly always sent out. Quickly I got ready. A leader approached me, "We have a lot of guests coming tomorrow evening and all the food needs to be prepared. Stay behind and work in the kitchen."

My heart sank. Oh no, how could this happen? I took off my coat and went into the kitchen. A whole sack of potatoes needed to be peeled. I stood at the sink and started washing the first lot. The other person in there was the one who had so bitterly chastised me over the communion service. Oh no this was going to be miserable. I felt like keeling over and crying. I was in utter despair. "Oh, God, oh Lord Jesus Christ, hear my prayer. If you really have more power than Sun Myung Moon then over-rule and deliver me. Last night a miracle took place and tonight is the last night of the Gospel Mission. Please do something. I must somehow get there."

I limply took a potato. The minibus engines started. The door opened. "Veronica is too ill to go out witnessing, she must be replaced. She can sit in here and peel the potatoes." A very exhausted and relieved Veronica sat at the kitchen table and took a potato. It was not a kindness I had seen before.

He pointed at me. "You will have to take her place, get a coat and get into the bus."

I ran to obey! Thank you, Lord Jesus!

As I sat on that bus my heart was beating wildly. What a wonderful God was this that He could turn things around in answer to prayer? Oh Jesus, I love you. Yet a great hurdle still lay before me. What if I was teamed with another more senior member as was usual? "Oh Jesus, please, cause me once again to be an odd one out."

I looked on the unhappy faces around me. I longed to tell them, but I dare not. There would be trouble and I would be sent straight back to the senior leader again. We sat in silence but this time I had a new and different God to pray to! One that really worked miracles and loved me.

We got out. Everyone teamed up. I was on my own again!

Amazing!

'Where did you go last night?" asked the leader. "A religious meeting on the Whitley Estate."

"Did you make any contacts there?"

"Yes."

"Can you follow them up again tonight?"

"Yes."

"Good – well go there then."

Thank you, Jesus! The Unification Church were actually sending me back themselves. Only God could do this.

And so that's how I came to go back to the Underwood Free Church on the evening of April 27th, 1972.

One and a half hours later after a beautiful service, a small, happy group of us sat on chairs in the vestry, with Pastor Ben Belsham kneeling, and I followed him in a prayer of repentance, renunciation of Sun Myung Moon and all The Unification Church stood for and of inviting Jesus Christ into my life!

Oh happy Day!
Oh happy Day!
When Jesus washed my sins away!

As I sat there, tears rolling down my cheeks, somewhere a great, huge old door swung open. Every lock undone. Brambles pushed aside, and through that door, light flooded into my soul and spirit and filling my very being. I had never known such light. The Light of the world, Jesus Christ, thorn-crowned and bleeding, had become my Lord and Saviour!

The choirs of heaven were singing – HALLELUJAH! She that was lost is found. Beth is saved!

Through An Open Door

After most people had gone home, a very happy and excited group of us sat around in Pastor Jim and Janet Morris's home. We had so much to talk about – the scriptures, Jesus' return, the power of prayer. How Jesus had reached every one of them. We laughed, prayed, talked and sang. Jim gave me a Gospel of John and as I read the first chapter I was bowled over by the power of the words. I couldn't wait to read it all! Jim also talked of the Baptism in the Holy Spirit and Ben explained that when he had prayed for me in a foreign language it was in fact the gift of speaking in tongues as explained in the book of Acts. Even as I sat talking, God baptized me in the Spirit that night.

Oh rapturous delight. Did ever such mortals know such joy? So this was the Good News that Jesus came to give us! Oh that the world would receive Him! His gospel could turn the world upside down.

After a while we realised it was 2:30 am. Some earnest thought had to be given to my future. Pastor Jim and Janet had a second evangelist staying in their spare room who was with us and he said that he'd move out and sleep on the sofa so that I could have his room. Jim and Janet immediately said, "Come and live with us." However I knew already in my heart what I must do. I must return home to my parents who had been so devastated by my leaving. Jim voiced his thoughts. "You need at least a week to stay with us. We have prayer gatherings and Bible studies and we can help to strengthen you for times ahead." It was a very wise suggestion.

Pastors Ben and Jim agreed that I should make my move out of the farm final, and go and collect my few last items. At 3 am they would still all be up, so we drove off in Ben's car. Ben and Jim couldn't believe the remoteness of the farm or the obvious hive of activity it was when we reached there at the dead of night.

Suddenly I felt uneasy. Who knew how the leaders would react to news of my leaving?

"You go in and we'll stay out here and pray," volunteered Ben. I hesitatingly got out of the car and slipped noiselessly in the back door. My new yellow case. Where was it? Hadn't it been taken down to the basement? I tiptoed nervously because all the boys slept down there. I found it amongst a pile of others. I stared at it. It was covered with foreign travel tickets. It had been taken to several countries in different parts of the world, though I never knew who had used it. I tiptoed upstairs, went along the back corridor and there stood a Family Member.

"What are you doing?" he said coldly. I wouldn't lie. "I'm leaving."

"I see," he stated, and disappeared.

Would he report me? Now I hurried to the attic, threw open my little drawer, stuffed my possessions in my case, grabbed a pair of shoes, a dress, snapped the case shut and turned around.

There, coming in the door, were Debbie and John. They carried two wooden chairs. They closed the door shut, placed the chairs hard against it and sat down and faced me. They did not look pleased. Oh no. What was I in for? Debbie looked from the case to me.

"What are you doing?"

"I'm leaving."

"Why?"

"I have become a Christian."

SILENCE. I really did feel afraid at that moment, when I declared that. But I felt in that instant I must take a stand for Jesus, I also believed that He had the power to deliver me.

"How did this happen?" in a voice like ice.

"I have been working for months at this farm, doing conditions, obeying the Law of Indemnity, making restitution, being chastised, fasting, praying, in order to reduce the great debt of my sins. Now I know that Jesus Christ died on the cross to pay the full price of my sin and I am set free and made completely whole, so there is no need for me to stay here any longer."

Debbie spoke in the kindest voice I had ever heard her use. "It is true that Jesus can forgive small everyday sins, God has allowed him this, but he cannot forgive original sin and this is the great barrier between us and God. It is for this reason that Master had to come. Only he can deal with the original sin. The Christians do not know this."

For a moment I was thrown. Oh no, what was the answer to this? Debbie actually looked ready to receive me forgivingly back!

In my mind I recalled John Shaw's face before me explaining so carefully that Jesus' death paid the full price of original sin.

Suddenly I was filled with a holy boldness only Jesus could have given me. "Jesus can forgive each one of us original sin. He has won the victory and triumphed over death and Satan. I have given my life to Jesus Christ and I believe in Him. He is the Almighty God and all power belongs to Him. I wish now to leave and follow Him."

Debbie's face was a picture. There was a harsher tone in her voice now. "You have listened to lies. You have played straight into Satan's hands and you will be cursed."

"Please may I leave?"

I turned to ensure my case was shut and to say a silent prayer.

When I turned around, all I saw was a wide open door. Debbie and the other leader were proceeding down the stairs, carrying their chairs. I stood astonished. Could this be true? Perspiration broke out on me. Was this something sinister or were they just letting me go?

With anxious steps I walked to the open door. Praying to Jesus, I walked through that door and to the other side. I continued to the landing and looked forward then down towards the back door; my path had been left clear. I gave one last look to the open door. It was such an incredible sight, and to this day I shall never forget just standing there and looking at it. How amazing! Jesus had just opened the way for me. Jesus had reached out to me through a vision of a door and now He literally and opened the way to my new found freedom.

I was back in the car. I threw the case in.

"Everything OK?"

"Yes, let's go!"

Revving up quietly, Ben swung the car back. Bang, the exhaust hit a rock and broke. We roared off like a jumbo jet. The whole community now heard my leaving and would undoubtedly soon hear of the reason! We could just hear above the din Ben reminding us of a scripture concerning the spread of the gospel, "and it was noised abroad." We all laughed. Hallelujah!

Goodbye Sun Myung Moon. Hello Jesus.

The Baptism

How I loved being a Christian! Every day became a pleasure to live through, and an adventure for Jesus. And friends! I never guessed there were so many born-again Christians, there were all the Whitley Estate Christians and then all the Fellowship at John and Marion Shaw's home. To think that we at Rowlane had thought we were the only God-fearers in all England! I met Christians on the bus to work and even at Courages Brewery.

Ah yes, Courages Brewery. They were amazed at the transformation in me and couldn't believe it. Mr. Mathews said that he had saved me, but of course I had to put him right on that. Mind you, he had been a very tolerant man! However, I began to feel unhappy about working for a brewery and asked the Lord to find me a new job – the one of His choice. I left Courages and went to an Agency who sent me to 183 King's Road, Reading – The Agricultural, Horticultural and Forestry Industry Training Board, (yes, I had to say all that on every phone call). It proved to be the ideal job for me. It was a beautiful office with modern lighting, over-looking a garden. There was a team of just eight of us and we worked very well together. One of their number had just left to be a full-time evangelist with The Good News Crusade. His name was Mike Darwood and he, with Don Double, were to evangelize all over England for many years. It was as if, in a sense, I stepped into his place. I was very happy there. I had learnt that when we commit our work to the Lord, He can bring us into His employment. When I was 21, they presented me with some beautiful Wedgewood pottery which still graces my mantleshelf to this day.

John and Marian Shaw's Fellowship (run with the indefatigable, loving character of Dave Medlock) said several believers were being baptized next Sunday and would I like to join them?

"Yes!"

So the next Sunday we drove up in cars to the banks of the River Thames! I couldn't believe they were actually baptizing in the river. We all got out and sang hymns along the riverbank (like in a Western). It was early May, and as the poet wrote, "May can be jolly cold in England" and it was. I looked at the swirling, cold, mud-coloured waters of Old Man Thames and I thought, "I can't do it. I'm going to freeze as soon as I'm knee deep. I will never be able to simply wade out, fully clothed, to chest high and be ducked under that water. I can't do it!" I don't like water at the best of times and I'm not a swimmer, but with about a hundred Christians present all singing God's praises it didn't look like there was a way out. How could I say I hadn't the courage to be baptized!?

"Please help me Lord, I need Your help and badly."

Two went before me and survived but they looked strong folk. It was my turn. In front of all those people I walked towards those waters, my eyes on John Shaw and Dave Medlock who were way out in the river. "Lord, help me."

I simply walked into and through that river and the water was warm. It was as lovely as a heated swimming pool. It was impossible ... but then hadn't I learnt that my God was the God of the impossible?

"Elizabeth, we baptize you in the Name of The Father, and of The Son and of The Holy Spirit."

Never was water so beautiful.

Deliverance

During that year I was invited to speak at countless gatherings and meetings. Reading had a lot of contact with the "Moonies" as people called them and they were ready to hear my story. Most lunch-times and after work I sought them out on the streets as they were witnessing and talked seriously to individuals, but it was like when Jackie had tried to talk to me all those months ago at Culham, unless the Lord opens a person's eyes they simply cannot see. I was reminded of Pastor Ben Belsham's words, "Talking will do no good, we must pray." Praise God, he had given me the gift of praying in tongues for my old Family colleagues and I saw a few of them come to faith in Jesus.

Time passed and I began to be aware of a curious thing. Whenever prayer meetings started I was hit by a headache. At first I ignored this, but it became too much of a coincidence. Every Thursday evening Pastor Jim and Janet invited me to dinner and to stay on for their Bible Study and I would stay the night there.

That Thursday I talked this over with them, and after prayer with some others they felt that I needed deliverance from forces of darkness that were still within me.

I was very taken aback and wasn't sure I liked the sound of this! However, since they had always been so kind and had been right on so many things, I agreed to go with them to a week-long "Come Back to God" Campaign Conference. The Campaign Team, led by the Rev. Dennis Paterson, and which had delegated Pastor Ben to lead the Mission in the Underwood Free Church, with the meetings that I have described, were pleased to hear that I would be joining them on one of their two annual Conferences.

When, after the Conference had begun and it was time for the Team to help me, Pastor Dennis, as the Team leader is usually known, asked Pastor Ben to take the lead in ministry to me since he had been instrumental in leading me to the Lord. One early evening there, Pastor Ben and Pastor Jim said that they had been asked to pray with me. I was still very sceptical, but told myself that, when nothing happened, then they would know.

A lot happened! When I arrived in the room about 10 persons were gathered, among them a nurse and an Anglican minister (just to observe)! Ben Belsham prayed firstly for protection of us all and our families, and that any spirits cast out would go where God sent them. He then lightly placed his hand on my shoulder and commanded in a soft and gentle voice that any unclean spirits within me were to leave now in the name of Jesus Christ.

Just for three seconds I thought nothing was going to happen. That was very short-lived. Suddenly four things happened at once. Firstly, a major activity started in my abdomen like things fighting and then they leaped up to my throat. Secondly, they started coming out of my mouth with high pitched screaming. Thirdly, I was thrown on to the floor and fourthly, my hands were both taken over and I began to strangle myself with my own hands!

Did I believe in demons? Well I did now! I realised that these were the same wretched things that manifested themselves wherever Jesus went. Jesus was present now and they were certainly manifesting themselves.

Two of the men instantly grabbed one of my arms each and with a lot of strength held my arms to stop me hurting myself. I never ceased to wrestle from them, neither did demon after demon cease to be expelled from my mouth. I was so embarrassed (I was wearing some nice evening clothes) that I tried desperately to speak to them, but speech was totally impossible since my voice box was no longer mine and the loud screaming continued.

After a few minutes I didn't feel I could physically keep this up and the Lord took over, and mercifully I lost consciousness. I came to at 2.30 am in the morning. I was still screaming, and I was aware that I was huddled in a ball in a dark, claustrophobic place. My arms were being pulled straight out either side of me while I still wrestled with all my might. The only faculty left to me was my mind, and praise God, it was still crystal clear. "Wherever am I?" I thought, "Surely this deliverance can't still be going on?" But it was.

By this time, Pastor Dennis had been called in to give advice and guidance. Someone said, "She's come around." Pastor Dennis then spoke up and said, "We will command the rest of the spirits to return to their present place and be bound until such time as they will be cast out," and this is the prayer he then prayed. (On page 77 I describe how they were all eventually expelled for good.) Immediately, the screaming stopped, I felt things sink back down my throat and into my abdomen again. My arms became my own again and I slowly crawled out of where I was – I had been huddled in a ball under the middle of a low double bed! They told me that that was where, even though unconscious, I had forced myself despite all their strength, and no one could get me out.

Those poor people had had to be up with me half the night. The Anglican minister looked washed out. But I was fine! My voice box had been used to its limits, but I could whisper my grateful thanks for their endurance for one awful night. The nurse went to bring us all a tray of tea and biscuits and everyone felt we should have a praise meeting. It was great! We sang and prayed and some prophesied under the anointing of the Holy Spirit (as told of in Acts).

What a celebration. What a victory! What a Great God!

It was gone 3 am before we got to bed. As I lay there in the dark, thinking it over, my arms throbbing, I realised that it was these deep, dark forces of evil that had led me to believe The Unification Church's doctrine and had driven me on so mercilessly while I was there. It was their voices that had kept speaking to me about Master and would have continued to do so until my death. The voices left me for good and I never had suicidal thoughts again.

People try to fight doctrines with words, but I believe we are dealing, as the Bible says, with the doctrines of demons. There is only one escape and that is to receive the Doctrine of Truth. Jesus said, "I AM the Way, the Truth and the Life. No one comes to the Father except through Me."

I thought of some of the rock stars I had previously idolised and how they would sometimes emulate these demons, being enthralled by the fascination and excitement. In reality there is no fun or excitement about these evil spirits, and I was realising the dangers of any dabblings with them at all.

God was teaching me many things and still had lessons to teach me on deliverance. When a host of demons come out of a person they have lived in for years, that is not always the end of the story. Jesus gives a warning when He related that when a demon comes out of a person, it travels around waterless places, looking for another home. If it finds no other home it joins up with other homeless spirits and remembers the home where it was expelled from. And, with the other spirits, it returns, just to see if by chance, that person has fallen away from the Lord and no longer has any defence. That spirit, and the others, can then re-enter. Jesus concludes, that in this case, the state of the person is worse than he was in the beginning. (Luke 11:24–26)

This warning had to be heeded. Pastors Jim Morris and Ben Belsham were right to wait for a full year before they cast demons out of me. Up until that time we had all prayed that they would be bound inside of me and they were. If they caused trouble, I bound them myself in Jesus' name straightaway. Jesus was always with me and He had all power over the enemy, so there was no need to rush off for deliverance. It could wait until the right time.

Another reason to wait was to give me a chance to cultivate a close relationship with the Lord through prayer, meditation on God's Word, fellowship with other believers and entering into the good works He called me to do, that His joy and life might flow through me to not only bless me, but make me a blessing to others. Then, when those demons would try to return one day, they would know pretty quickly that they didn't stand a chance and they would flee. Praise God.

Six months later I was to experience the night the demons tried to return!

The Counterattack

After I'd been a Christian for 18 months, I sensed the Lord's leading to go Christian Life College in Dorset. This was a big step for me at the time but I was excited about it. I was sorry to say goodbye to Jim and Janet especially as they had been so very good to me and had bought me a beautiful Bible which I use to this day. It's very worn and dog-eared and greatly underlined. They have never failed to write to me through all these years. The College was run by Elmer and Jean Darnall, and guest speakers taught us each week-day evening. In the daytime we found employment in order to support ourselves and also to make sure we didn't become a holy huddle of believers! They had come over from America and Jean's enthralling story was told in her book *Heaven Here I Come* (Lakeland). A dynamic couple, they are in their seventies now and are still ministering and linked to Youth With A Mission. Only God can make people in their seventies still young.

While I was there, I lodged with a cheerful family, Phil and Carolyn Runciman, who had previously been students at the College. One weekend they were away, and I was left alone in the house. All went fine until the evening came and I gradually began to feel very uneasy. Something was going to happen and I didn't know what. The feeling continued so strongly that I felt I must prepare myself. I started praying for my protection and took the Bible and it fell open at Psalm 91. I read it and clung to every word.

"He who dwells in the shelter of the Most High ... in the shadow of the Almighty ... will say, 'My Refuge and my Fortress.'" I made sure every door and window was locked. I turned off the lights and trod nervously up the stairs. What was it? Why did I have this strange, disturbed feeling?

As I entered my room, I suddenly remembered that Rex Meakin had taught us at College earlier in the day, and he had told us about some Christians who had bought a house to discover it had been used previously by spiritualists. They had felt God lead them to carefully tread out the perimeter of every room and to claim the ground for Jesus and to remind the devil of the blood that Jesus shed in His victorious triumph over sin and Satan's power. Their scripture they took from Joshua 1:3.

It occurred to me that this was exactly what I should do now around my room. Never did anyone so carefully pace, toe to heel around a room (even furniture was moved and put back) and pray so diligently, as I did that evening! Finally, I sat on my bed. Why had I felt so strongly that I must do this? It was an uncanny feeling and I can't explain it.

Trembling about the unknown night ahead, I shut the door. It didn't lock. I got into bed and turned off the light.

Zim! Wham! What was that! I woke up abruptly. What followed next may be very, very hard for you to believe. But although I had no witness, I can testify that every word is true.

I sat in the pitch black, already in a cold sweat. I could sense sinister evil. Suddenly I could see on another dimension and flying through the black, night air were literally thousands of horrific demons. The night was charged with hideous, dynamic evil forces. Even as they flew through the air, further demons were joining them, and their host was growing in number until from a distance they were like a huge, ominous black cloud of ravens. They may have been miles away when I first saw them, but they flew quickly and were coming nearer and nearer. I sat petrified, because I knew, without shadow of doubt, that they were heading for me, and that they hated me and wanted my death. "Oh Lord, Lord. Help me! Come to my rescue quickly!"

Lines of Psalm 91 flew to my mind "You will not fear the terror of the night ... nor the pestilence that marches in darkness."

Suddenly they rammed the house and were coming through the walls into the kitchen downstairs. How so many thousands jammed in I don't know, but still they came through the walls.

For one fearful moment all was quiet as they marshalled themselves. Then it happened. With one accord they sprang like lightning through the corridor, up the stairs and to my room and wham! They were knocked back! They picked themselves up and hurtled themselves at the walls and door again, but again they were knocked back. Their anger knew no bounds and I could see their contorted faces and hear their enraged screams.

Sitting terrified in a cold pool of sweat I realised that the walls and door were holding because I had trodden them round, claiming the power of Jesus' blood, the night before. The demons couldn't stand it! Their fury unleashed itself for the next two hours against that wall and door. All the while I constantly prayed and verses of Psalm 91 came to me again and again.

> A thousand may fall at your side, ten thousand at your right hand, but it will not come near you.

I hung onto those words like a dying man. If they should get through? What then? Would I survive?

> Because you have made the Lord your refuge ... no evil shall befall you... He will give His angels charge over you.

At times I saw the wooden door bow right inwards with the power and force of their fists and feet, but it never gave way. At times I thought my ear drums would split with the pitch of their screams.

> You will tread on the lion and the adder ... the serpent you will trample underfoot.

Then suddenly – SILENCE. Utter and complete silence.

I held my breath. I could still see them clearly. They were just standing there, defeated and broken. Then one gave a signal. They raised themselves and turned with the same lightning speed that they had come as they fled, far into the night sky.

> "Because he cleaves to Me in love, I will deliver him. I will protect him, because he knows My Name. When he calls to Me, I will answer him, I will be with him in trouble, I will rescue him and honour him." (Psalm 91)

I sat dripping with sweat in bed, a shaking jelly, but a loving peace and the knowledge of God's mighty power was around me.

Jesus said, "I AM THE DOOR." I had learnt that He can open a rusted, locked door of many years and He can also bar shut against all forces, a door that hasn't even got a lock.

As I sit writing this many years later, I would like to tell you that never again has any attack like that come near me. Those demons must have a good memory!

From Dorset To London

In the first year of my conversion I had been praying once in my bedroom and had turned to the parable of the Wedding Feast. All the rich and honoured guests had been invited and everyone refused. Finally the Host said, "Well the banquet is all laid and prepared, go and bring in the poor, the blind and the lame from the highways and the byways that my banqueting hall may be filled." I felt the Lord speaking to me and saying that all respectable and decent people in this world are invited yet most of them refuse to come. "I will send you to the back streets and byways of the city to bring in the poor, the blind and the lame." "Where will this be?" I wondered. The answer seemed to be with me even as I asked: "London." I kept this secretly within my heart, not knowing how it would ever come about, but often mulling it over.

I had been at Christian Life College in Dorset only two months when Jean Darnall spoke to us all one evening and said that much as she loved the beauty of the Dorsetshire countryside, God had been speaking to her and telling her that His heart lay with the rejected and outcasts of the streets of London. There were many now who lived on the streets, homeless, alcoholic, drug users, many from broken homes, or who had never even known a home, or a father. "God loves these people," Jean went on, "and while they are lying on the streets of London we can't stay here."

And so our move to London came about. A friendly student I had got to know well, Carol Goldsmith, had come from London and offered me then and there accommodation at her flat in Stoke Newington, North London. Praise the Lord for this provision. Carol had been delivered from spiritualism and between us we had plenty to share!

An Anglican minister, Nicholas Rivett-Carnac of St Mark's Church, Kennington, in notorious South-East London, heard of Christian Life College's desired move to London, and together with a Christian businessman, offered the rental of the spacious first floor of his large church. It was God's provision and, with the college and church combined, an immense amount of outreach and ministry was to go out to the surrounding area for over a decade. Many were converted and delivered. Sir Nicholas Rivett-Carnac's own remarkable story was told in his book *Upon This Rock* (Hodder & Stoughton). He was an English gentleman, in every sense, who gave up the life he could have had, to serve the poor and needy on London's back streets for many years.

I arrived alone at Paddington Railway Station with my smart mustard yellow suitcase. I now had to travel through the tubes. I didn't realise that I had arrived in the rush-hour. The tube platform was packed! The tube hurtled in, screeching. The doors flew open and it was jam-packed inside! "That's it," I thought, "no one can get on." Wrong. The crowd surged forward and a few hundred people pushed themselves on. The doors snapped shut on them and hurtled off, leaving those of us that were left in a howl of cold, rushing wind. The next tube came in. The same experience. Off it thundered into a black hole.

"Please, please, help me, Lord, I don't think I can ever get on one of those tubes." And yet I had no alternative.

The next packed tube hurtled in with a roar. The doors whizzed open and again it was packed. Like I walked to my baptism, so I walked to those doors in a sea of people. "Go in My Name, My child, I am with you." With a few hundred others, we pushed and squeezed ourselves into a resisting dense body of people. With a suitcase it was doubly hard. The doors slammed. The engines roared and we were off. I had never experienced anything like it before. At each station about three people got off and a hundred got on. I began to panic. We could hardly breathe. Surely this couldn't go on? No one spoke, they only pushed like machines. Not a flicker of expression on a face. Jolt, the doors squealed open and another hundred people surged forward. By this time, I couldn't believe that the train would ever hold us, or that I would ever get out.

My panicking eyes saw a man with a large suitcase looking desperate in this suffocating and hopeless situation. Astonishingly I felt that I could help him and with my eyes I motioned to him to come over to me. As he pushed towards me, I lifted my case from the floor space it took and indicated to him to put his case there. I then balanced my case on my feet. I caught a glimpse of thankful relief on his face and I turned away. I was stricken. By now I had lost all count of how many stations we had passed and when I needed to get out. It didn't seem possible to see any station names above the sea of heads. The whole thing was a living nightmare and I hadn't even arrived.

"Lord, Help me!"

Several stops later I actually glimpsed my destination. The opposite doors slammed open. I was on the wrong side! No one wanted to get off and a hundred looked ready to surge on. Sheer panic and horror filled me. I had to get off and it was purely impossible. In a hopeless attempt I tried to push forward. The stranger I had beside me observed my weak attempt.

Suddenly he shouted at the full volume of his lungs. "Make way! Make way for the lady. This woman is a lady. I tell you that when I came on this train nobody wanted me and nobody helped. You all turned away, but this woman, when she saw me, she made space for my case. Make way! Make way!"

For a second everyone froze, including me. I couldn't believe it. And then suddenly the Red Sea parted and a huge gangway appeared before me as everyone on instant reflex pressed back. The people surging on also stopped and all pushed back. I stood utterly shocked and every eye was on me, He turned to me and said, "Walk this way, lady, and go your way."

I picked up my case and walked through the aisle. I stood on the platform and looked back. Everyone remained where they were and looked at me and as the doors closed, I heard the man start to shout the tale again.

I stood on that platform by a miracle of God. Dazed. What an amazing thing. Whether that stranger was of an earthly or heavenly order I never knew, but he was an instrument of God that day.

God had opened a door; he had kept a door shut, and now He had done the impossible again – He had kept slamming, automatic doors open until I walked through.

Staying with Carol and her flat mates was a great joy. They were all nurses and worked at St. Bartholomew's Hospital that had an enormously large and strong Christian Union (bigger than most church fellowships). Carol took me along and even set me up with a secretarial post there. I was also greatly intrigued by the Orthodox Jews walking everywhere in Stoke Newington with long flowing robes and beards. My heart went out to them and I longed for them to come into the fullness of their glorious Messiah. I spent time praying for them and wondered if God would ever use me to somehow reach them. I didn't know then that my father came from a Jewish family. He had fought against Hitler in the Second World War and had kept his Jewishness to himself. I had distant memories of an elderly grandmother whose mind had gone, and who had rambled on about terrible things.

Days flew by, everyone in Carol's lively flat was so kind and God's blessings were all around, but I had a very heavy heart. I came from the country and I simply couldn't face the long tube journeys every evening to Kennington and back.

I began to pray that God would find me accommodation and employment within walking distance of St. Mark's Church so that I wouldn't have to use any London transport! I still hadn't seen Kennington and talked to Carol about it. She looked very doubtful. "Kennington's an unusual place. It's one of the poorer parts of London, and yet you can turn off into a side road and find yourself unexpectedly in a select road of gracious residences, still standing as it were from a bygone era, when places like Kennington, Brixton and Vauxhall were well-to-do areas. However, a lot has changed and a vast amount of today's Kennington consists of large blocks of council flats or tenement brick buildings, blackened by years of London's grime and pollution. Thousands of needy and underprivileged families now live there. There's a high alcoholic and crime rate and only a few brave shop-keepers and businesses." Carol considered my naive and trusting country ways. "You need to be quite street-wise to live there and to be honest I think it's very doubtful you'd find anywhere to live, let alone any employment." The others all agreed. Carol was a very good friend and I weighed her words carefully. I churned it all over and continued praying.

There were only two days to go before Christian Life College started and I braved the journey down to Kennington. When I arrived, my eyes beheld some of the dreariest streets I had ever seen. No bright coloured neon lights shone out here. As small as I felt, a sense of God's calling quickened within me. People's faces everywhere told a story of depression and dismal hopelessness.

I saw a man lying flat on the dirty pavement. I went straight to him gently shaking him and asking him if there was anything I could do. A stream of abuse was my reward; I backed away. For the four years I remained there I never saw a happy face, unless it was the face of a Christian, and then there was great joy and happiness, fun and laughter. People at large don't realise the JOY that God brings when you know Him!

"Lord, here I come, please provide that job and accommodation."

Within the hour I was to have both.

I called in at St Mark's Church and they told me that a Christian family, who lived almost opposite in one of those few gracious roads, had come in a few days before and offered accommodation for one single girl student. It was the only offer of accommodation made to Christian Life College. I went straight there, and we met each other and came to an arrangement over a lovely, newly decorated Laura Ashley room! I was to share the top landing with the nanny, Rosemary, the daughter of missionaries to Nepal.

The only concern they showed was when I said that I had no employment. They seemed hesitant on this point, but I told them not to worry, if I could just leave my case there, I'd be back in an hour after I had found a job. They looked even more worried. Like Carol, they knew the district.

I left and just walked where my feet led me. I saw a tiny little sort of shop that had so many barricades and bars across its small windows that I approached it mainly out of curiosity just to see if it really was a shop. Then I saw that a part of one of the small windows was covered with postcards selling items for people. I scanned them. One said "WANTED – TYPIST – CHURCH OF ENGLAND'S CHILDREN'S SOCIETY, OLD TOWN HALL, KENNINGTON."

Asking a passer-by, I discovered it was just down the road. I went straight there, saw the likeable Manager, John Cope, and was taken on to start the next day. I was to remain there for a long time and had much pleasure in working there and always joined in the morning prayer meetings stipulated by the founder Edward Rudolf. The heroic story of it all, much of it set in Kennington and the East End of London, over 150 years ago, is set out in his book *13 Penny Stamps*, and I considered it a privilege to be involved in the continuance of that work long after his death. The Old Town Hall was a very old building and I discovered that when it had become redundant it hadn't been known what to do with it and eventually it had been offered to the Children's Society. It was an appropriate district for it and they did tremendous work.

What wonderful provision all round! God had done it again! When we go somewhere for Jesus' sake, and trust in Him, there is nothing that He cannot do. No door that He cannot open.

That first year at Christian Life College was filled with the pleasure of knowing and serving Jesus and being part of Elmer and Jean Darnall's Bible College and ministry. Many people's lives were deeply influenced for Christ and others found hope and healing and a new life for the first time.

The Miracles Continue

For the summer break I returned home to Upton, Berkshire to be with my family. I knew how much Mum and Dad loved to have me around. My brother, Laurie, became a Christian, which was very exciting, and we talked for hours.

That summer we went with a local church to the Festival of Jesus. It was a huge week-long rally held in London. It was fantastic to see London alive for Jesus with hundreds of thousands of Christians holding mass rallies every day. I was in the seventh heaven all week long.

A small convoy of us went in cars through endless London roads to a church hall where we unpacked, made tea and excitedly chatted. Neither Laurie nor I took the slightest notice of where we actually were. Then we all packed into cars again, parked and walked to Hyde Park Corner. Hundreds of thousands of Christians gathered that day and when Cliff Richard sang on a high platform "Jesus, Jesus, Won't You Come Back To Earth?" I was ecstatic with happiness. Jean Darnall spoke and inspired that whole crowd afterwards. It was while she was speaking that I looked around and noticed something. A huge and massive circle of witches had surrounded us. They stood with arms outstretched, touching fingertip to fingertip, dressed in long dark cloaks covered in ominous signs, with matted hair and glaring faces painted dramatically in white inverted crosses. Immediately my heart went out to them, slaves to a punishing Master. I walked as quickly as I could to the first one and started to tell her of the love of Jesus and of His death and blood shed for her. Immediately something happened. Her defiant face changed into one of misery and then terrible fear. She threw herself at my feet and started to wriggle on the ground. I threw myself on the ground and joined her and proceeded to tell her of the delivering power of Jesus Christ. The terror on her face I have only seen once since. Suddenly she jumped up and ran like lightning from Hyde Park. The circle had been broken, I looked at the other witches but they seemed to be melting. I looked once at Jean Darnall and then I looked again at the witches and everyone had gone.

What a pity they had so hardened their hearts, but demons flee when they come into the presence of the gospel and often they carry the person with them.

When that happy day was finally all over in Hyde Park, Laurie had got completely separated from any of us. He searched and searched but couldn't find us, and we searched too. Finally we decided that he would make his own way back. That would have been fine, but Laurie had no inkling of where we were in all London, the name of the church hall, or any money. There really was nothing he could do but pray and so that is what he did!

He stayed for hours just hoping he might still see one of us and gradually it came to night fall. An elderly, kindly couple, the sort that had waited all their lives to see this day and didn't want to leave, were just starting to wend home. Laurie felt drawn to them and approaching them he asked if he could have a lift with them. "Where are you going?" they asked.

That was the tricky part. Laurie had to explain. "If you could just drive through London to where you are going, I'll look out the window and I may recognise something." It was a remote chance, but this kindly couple agreed. They set off.

After about 30 minutes Laurie saw all our cars outside the church hall and our church group walking about. "I'm here," he shouted, and the couple set him down. They were as surprised as Laurie. Aware of how vast London is the miracle has never ceased to amaze me!

Another day he drove me to a large Crusade in a major Oxford Hall to hear a well-known evangelist. When we arrived, there was a big notice to say that the evangelist was ill and that a Fred Smith would take his place! I was so disappointed. Fred gave a quiet, simple gospel message and then asked if anyone would like to come forward to receive the Lord as Saviour, or simply for a touch from Him. No one moved in that vast hall. He repeated the invitation three times and there was no response. I stood up. I couldn't let this happen. Never let it be said that no one responded. So despite my disappointment, in front of all those people I walked alone down the aisle to the waiting Fred Smith. But Jesus Christ is never a disappointment. Behind me, lots of people started to arise and follow. Fred started ministering down the line.

"Father, I don't know what my need is, but whatever it is, please minister to me, and meet that need." It was hot and humid in there, but a rushing wind started to blow around my head, round and round. I remembered the day of Pentecost when the wind of the Holy Spirit blew around a room. It was the same rushing wind and then words were spoken to me out of the wind. "I will deliver you, I will deliver you, I will deliver you." When Fred was about two people away from me a strong activity started in my abdomen and something sprang at my throat and I began retching. Fred came over and simply said, "Come out of her, come out of her," and that was it. Right there in front of all those people those demons that had been left inside of me, came out screaming. Fred seemed quite used to it and quickly gave me his own large handkerchief. They were gone! I was delivered! What a surprise! The demons never returned.

Shortly before I returned to London, I was alone in our out-lying country home which was surrounded by a large, quarter acre garden. The lights were on but I had not drawn the blinds. I was backwards and forwards from the front dining room to the back kitchen clearing the table and washing up. My hands were deep in the hot water when a clear inner voice spoke to me, "Get down on your knees and pray." It seemed without purpose and I carried on. "Get down on your knees and pray."

"I can't," I thought, "or I won't get this washing up done." "Get down on your knees and pray." I felt that this was something irrational. It sounded like the Lord's voice, but surely He didn't tell you to do things when there was no reason. "Get down on your knees and pray." The voice was firm and insistent. I was worried, the voice was continuous now. I reasoned that if I got down and prayed for about two minutes, I could get up again and I would have done it.

I went into the front room, where there was an open window to the hot, balmy, summer evening, and knelt near it on the soft carpet. What would I pray? The instant I got down on my knees and began to pray, all heaven opened. Angels surrounded me and I was taken up into heavenly realms in the spirit, far above this world. I was filled with sheer joy and happiness. I joined a heavenly choir and sang the Almighty God's praise. Worship in English and in tongues poured from my mouth. There seemed no song I couldn't sing. It was the most glorious thing I had ever experienced, and it went on and on. I never wanted it to finish.

Prayer flowed from my lips and the Lord was filling my mouth with words. How long this went on I don't know for time glided into eternity. It was possibly an hour.

Suddenly it came to an abrupt end with loud shouting within three feet of me. My father's voice, "Who are you and what are you doing?" A fight started right there on the path just outside the open window. I ran to the window and my Dad was wrestling with a man on the ground. The man shook free and ran like lightning into the darkness. Dad gave chase but it was no good. My parents raced in, wondering what ordeal I had been through, but praise the Lord, I had never even seen him.

So, a man had stood watching me at the open window all the time. What were his intentions? The hand of the Lord had stayed him and prevented me from even seeing him in a most unusual way. Thank goodness I had, at last, obeyed the Lord's command. Supposing I hadn't?

I hoped that the next time His voice spoke to me so urgently, I would be much quicker to respond, but, almost tragically, I was slow to respond on another, even more dangerous, occasion in London.

Bring In The Poor, The Blind And The Lame

In September I returned to London for the Second Year of Christian Life College. Another student, a widow of sixty, asked me to come and share her flat. I hesitated. How would we get on? I was a lively 24-year-old and she was, well sixty. I need not have worried. God was in charge! Ena Allwright was a dynamic, big-hearted, vivacious Christian. In her words, she had lived over 40 years in the wilderness before coming to know Christ and she wasn't going to waste a minute now. I must say that I never knew her to waste a second. She rose at 5:30 am and had an hour of prayer from 6–7 am every morning, worked all day, cooked us a meal and then telephoned someone while she ate her meal and then off we went to Christian Life College for the evening. Sylvia Thomas, another Christian Life College student, came to join us and life was busy with Christian Life College three evenings a week, and the other evenings were a round of prayer meetings, guests for meals, missionary meetings, prayer for Israel, rehearsals for Messianic Jewish music groups (Jews who had come to know the Lord Jesus), Intercessors for Britain and film shows. On top of that we assisted at Jean Darnall's big meetings at weekends. Really there wasn't time for church(!) but of course we went, and it was always a great privilege to hear Nicholas Carnac ministering at St. Mark's Church. Many needy people flocked to that church and sometimes I would stay behind with Nicholas to pray with him for those who stayed behind for ministry.

The course at Christian Life College was coming to an end. The students would be going their separate ways. It had been a tremendous two-year course with hand-picked teachers by Elmer. Eric Lipson, an elderly Messianic Jew, and his wife Irene, had taught us many deep insights into the Old Testament, the Tabernacle and the Passover Meal. I was not to realise how important this would all mean to me until much later. What was I to do now? I started to pray every night for guidance. "Lord, you have been with me so much during these two years with Christian Life College. I long to be in your service, where will you send me?"

The Lord's answer came and was most unexpected. Nicholas Carnac had a very full-time ministry: as well as leading a large church where the Holy Spirit was allowed full sway and engaging in continual ministries and outreaches, he also taught Genesis at Christian Life College and ministered to all the down and outs at his vicarage on The Oval.

Two hundred and fifty years ago John and Charles Wesley and George Whitfield, those tireless, amazing evangelists who turned dark England upside down, would preach to hundreds of thousands week by week at Kennington's Oval. One hundred and fifty years ago William and Catherine Booth had done the same and thousands of hopeless lives were transformed.

Now Kennington Oval was a cricket ground, surrounded by countless large council tenement houses where thousands lived. Alcoholics slept on dreary cold pavements or packed out a nearby disused marmite factory for the night. A new generation was without hope.

Nicholas Rivett-Carnac now worked there, equally tirelessly. He had heard God's calling to seek the poor, the blind and the lame and to bring them into God's banqueting house. Nicholas opened up his door daily to give out endless drinks and sandwiches, invite people in for meals and personal talks and would even take some in to live with him that they might know Christ, the hope of this world.

Nicholas was praying for a housekeeper and felt God's guidance to ask me. I sensed God's affirmation, especially as I remembered a long time ago, the Lord had spoken to me and given me this very calling. "Go out and bring in the poor, the blind and the lame from the highways and the byways of the city." Now I was to go and join Nicholas and the rest of his small team at the vicarage.

What a ministry and what a God! Day after day people sought out the church and the vicarage and lives were healed and changed. The hopeless found hope, the sorrowful found joy and the hungry found food. The whole ministry was a challenge every day. There were sometimes mistakes and failures, but I can't remember many, and nothing that love and humour did not cover. The other vicarage team members were all completely committed to the work and God molded us together to daily put the needs of others before ourselves. Some worked full-time in outside jobs, giving in all their wages to pay the running costs, and receiving the £3 pocket money with the rest of us. It was a tremendous privilege to be part of such a work. The hours we kept would be very late, often one of was still talking and praying with someone in the early hours of the morning with our Bibles open. I remember two young men, Bob Bruce and Marshall Green, giving themselves tirelessly in this manner while I was there.

Although there were a lot of comings and goings we would meet for a house meeting with Nicholas once a week at around 10 pm to pray and share over the current guests we had staying and to share what we felt God was saying about each individual and how we should continue. This kept a close unity between us all. High priority was always given to prayer meetings with some rising with Nicholas at 6 am!

Angel Unaware

One day I had had to go out and came back thoroughly and utterly exhausted. I felt that as soon as I reached the vicarage, though it would be filled with needy people, I would have to wend myself to the kitchen and make myself a cup of tea and sit down for the first ten minutes. That was a very difficult thing to do at the vicarage. I had known an occasional team member sneak out to a local cafe to get a quiet cup of tea, but even there they'd discover themselves beside a needy soul and would eventually bring them back to the vicarage.

On this occasion, even as I approached the vicarage, the door opened and Graham Ashdown, one of the team, talked to me in the hallway. "Liz, there is a woman vagrant here who has nowhere else to sleep. Can she sleep with you in your little room tonight?"

I felt ready to collapse and I had continually shared rooms with needy people and then for the first time that night I was going to start sleeping in a little room downstairs by myself by the front door. I felt ready for it – and now this! My mind reeled. It was the limit of my physical endurance. Or was it?

In that instant a verse of scripture was spoken to me, not by any human voice, "Do not neglect to show hospitality to strangers, for thereby some have entertained angels unawares."

The scripture was so clear that I looked up and simply said "Yes, of course." Graham said, "Oh good, I knew you'd say that and I've already made her up a makeshift bed in your room." Just then the woman in question came and looked at me, "It'll only be for one night."

"That's all right," I replied, "you can stay as long as you like." With the scripture had come God's grace.

I then made my cup of tea and sat down, and the woman and I talked.

That night we laid in our beds talking till 3 am. The woman turned out to be a person with an incredible story. Coming originally from a wealthy, elite home in France, her small brother had been kidnapped.

Although a high ransom had been paid the boy had never been returned but rumour indicated he had been abandoned in England. Jean showed me old newspaper cuttings and photos which verified the story. She had walked the streets of London for years, becoming a reclusive vagrant, believing that amongst all London's hundreds of down-and-outs she would one day see him. She ate only in run-down cafes where she would sit smoking for hours. In one of these cafes, one of our team had gone (for a quiet cup of tea) and sat by her. He shared the love of Jesus with her and in that cafe, Jean Davids gave her life to Christ.

The next night, Jean was still sleeping in my room. After we had talked for hours, we eventually fell asleep, but fitfully, because in the pitch black I could hear a dull, continuous scraping sound. What was it? It seemed to come from the window, but I knew it was closed. Tiredness overtook me, but the scraping and scratching penetrated my dreams.

Suddenly, Jean was shouting and fighting with a man by the window. "Liz, Liz, turn on the light!" I was still very new to the room and couldn't find the switch in the dark. Wherever was it?

Still Jean fought on. "Call the others, get the others down!"

I ran out into the darkness. "Help, Help, Help, somebody come quickly. A man has broken into our room. Help, Help." I screamed, I shouted, I yelled. No one came. No one heard. I ran back and actually found the light switch and turned it on.

Bedazzled by the light and hearing the uproar the man decided to flee. He jumped back on to the window, well assisted by Jean, who told him in no uncertain terms to "Get out and be gone!".

What a night! I shook for a week afterwards. Because of Jean's years of living rough and fending for herself against numerous assaults she was not afraid to confront the strongest of men. I remembered the scripture the Lord had given me. How important it had been for me to show that hospitality. It had not only provided a refuge for Jean but protection for me.

I realised that there was another lesson here for all of us. Sometimes we feel at the end of our endurance – we feel we can't take any more. Just then God speaks a scripture to our heart which pleads with us to go yet another second mile.

We sometimes don't want to hear that voice, but when the Lord speaks a scripture (or a word) to us, He also gives the grace and strength to carry it through, very often quite supernaturally, and His reward comes with it. Sometimes that reward is our very life!

That day Jesus' words suddenly seemed very real: "If any man would come after Me, let him deny himself and take up his cross and follow Me. For whoever would save his life will lose it, and whoever loses his life for My sake will find it. For what will it profit a man, if he gains the whole world and forfeits his soul? And what shall a man give in return for his soul?" (Mark 8:37)

Jean was to become a firm friend and stayed on to help us with our ministry. She knew only too well the problems that faced people. One Sunday evening we all went to the evening service, except Jean. She was very perplexed because all afternoon she had felt that God was telling her not to go! We came to the eventual conclusion, that strange as it seemed, she should obey what she felt God was saying. Later, while Jean was sitting alone in the vicarage she heard a noise and discovered an intruder was breaking in. Jean lost no time in confronting him and sending him on his way! It made for a lot of conversation with the usual numbers of people that we brought back from church for coffees and hot chocolate.

I wish you could all have heard Jean sharing with us that evening on how important it is to listen to what God is saying to us. I remember her sitting there in a worn black dress, with her bare feet stuck in an old pair of men's shoes laced up with string and telling us that we can often hear four voices speaking to us – our own reasoning, the voices of those around us, the devil's voice, but most importantly, the voice of the Lord. His still small voice can, surprisingly, speak to us above all the clamour of the other voices. It proved a deeply moving time, and as we sat around the coffee table in the fading light, several needy people shared their longings to know God's voice above all the world's clamour. It was one of many holy and sacred evenings in the vicarage when we felt Jesus stop by. Soon Nicholas joined us and once again we all sensed God's power and presence with us in the discussion and prayer time that followed. I wish you could have been there with us that hot, summer evening. Consider yourself present. Consider yourself at home!

Someone drew out a guitar and led us in a beautiful rendering of, "The day Thou gavest Lord is ended ..."

Lives were changing and God's kingdom was still extending here on earth, using the weakest of us as we offered Him our availability.

God's Protection

Every now and again I went home to see my parents and even these trips could be fraught with danger as these next two incidents show, and we always made it a habit to pray that the Lord would keep us safe.

During the 1970s, the IRA held a bombing campaign in London. For this reason my parents were always very worried about my being there but I was always confident that the Lord would protect me, and He did.

One evening I was travelling to my parents' home by tube and knew I was going to face the evening rush hour (but by this time I had got used to it and hung from a strap attached from the roof crushed in with everyone else). I joined a queue that was so long it went outside the station door and down the pavement. From the time of joining that queue a small voice spoke to me and simply said, "Get a bus." I ignored it. It continued. I couldn't see that it made any sense. "Get a bus." I simply didn't want to; the buses were infrequent and irregular. Masses surged forward when the bus came in and more than once I had been fleeced of all my money in such surges. Tired and frustrated bus conductors would barricade the way before you could get on, shouting, "No more, no more," and the bus would speed off.

Usually at least one desperate person ran and hung on to the middle pole and ducked under the conductor's arms. I knew I couldn't attempt that with my yellow case! You can tell how bad the buses were to make me endure a rush hour tube journey from South to North London going right through the heart of the city.

"Get a bus." I would have to ignore it.

"Get a bus." I was half-way up the queue now.

"Get a bus." I would never catch the Paddington connection.

"Get a bus." "Get A Bus." "GET A BUS!" The voice was becoming louder and urgent.

"GET A BUS!!" My head reeled. "I can't, not now. I'm only two people to go."

"GET A BUS!!" I began hyperventilating. I could hardly breathe; it was like a panic attack.

I was one person to go.

The Lord spoke to me one last time: "GET A BUS." I looked at the gaping escalator going down into the depths, I saw the tired ticket seller look at me waiting and I stepped out of the line, walked to the dirty wall and leaned in a daze against it. I battled to get my breath. Already the next person was being served and the queue had tightened up. You don't leave a queue and get back in it in London. I would get a bus. For the first time the voice stopped. I walked in a daze to the bus stop. Straightaway a bus came in and I got on; there was even space for my case. I began to be aware something specific was happening. This was unusual. I even remember sitting next to a kindly Italian lady who noticed I couldn't catch my breath and who made friendly conversation. My breathing gradually returned to normal. Why was all this happening?

The big black Paddington train stood hissing and roaring at the platform and I jumped on. "Great. I'm on. Praise you Lord!"

I didn't realise just how much I should be thankful to God until I finally reached my home in Upton. There we all stood in horror and aghast at the scenes on the TV news.

That evening, the IRA planted a major bomb in an underground tube station, and it did what evil minds planned it would do – it caused a terrifying explosion in a packed carriage injuring many, some seriously. It was exactly where I would have been if I had not taken the bus. I stood numb. I thought of all those innocent people who had endured hours of a living nightmare before they could be brought to the surface. How I felt that night, I cannot describe.

Only the Lord had saved me. I felt utterly broken as I looked at the scenes and thought of how I had been so slow to heed God's warning voice, had put up every excuse and very nearly didn't heed the voice at all. I had so nearly bought my ticket and joined the crush of humanity down the long dark escalators.

May this experience speak to us all. How many times does God speak to us and we don't listen, or we let our own reasoning overrule? Commit your way to the Lord, and if you hear an inner voice directing you, follow it.

There came another time when I was in danger, and I thank God that this time I was quicker to obey His voice.

Again, I had been home and was returning to the vicarage after nightfall. The Oval was not a safe place to walk to, especially carrying a conspicuous yellow case, so I hailed a taxi to drive me there. The taxi driver dropped me as close as he could, and I paid him. The night was black, and I bent to pick up my case and bag and turn towards the vicarage. Just then a man stepped out in front of me and stood barring my way. His eyes ran over my bag and case and back to my face.

In that moment the Lord spoke to me, "This man wants to attack you for your bags. Chat and talk lightly to him."

I felt no fear and instantly obeyed the Lord. I made a friendly conversation and the man visibly relaxed and chatted pleasantly back.

"I will have to go now, as I am already late," I smiled after a few minutes, and turned to walk forwards and he let me pass.

"TURN AROUND," said an inner voice strongly.

I did so and the man was right behind me about to grab me. The Lord spoke to me again to engage the man in light conversation. I lost no time in obeying and again he chatted pleasantly back.

"Well, I really must go now," I laughed and again he let me pass. I made it four steps nearer to the vicarage.

"TURN AROUND!" This time the man was losing no time. He lurched towards me and with a grimace grabbed my coat collar and pulled me towards him. In that moment I cried out in my mind, "Jesus, help me." In that same instant the man stopped and looked over my shoulder. He saw something that terrified him for he gasped and reeled backwards. I stared at the terrified look on his face. He began to shield his face and look totally alarmed, then next moment he was on the ground at my feet and still staring above my shoulder.

I knew no fear and was completely transfixed. Then suddenly he sprang up and ran. He ran like a streak of lightning and I stood watching till he was out of sight. It was such an amazing sight. I looked behind me but there was no one there. I was completely alone, but I believe that an Angel had stood there behind me, guarding me, protecting me.

And so He will protect you too when you trust in the Lord with all your heart and follow after Him.

"For He will give His Angels charge over-you, to bear you up, lest you dash your foot against a stone." (Psalm 91:12)

What an adventure with and for Jesus I was being led into. I was still learning, and He was teaching me that if I followed Him with all my heart and placed my trust in Him He would never fail me nor forsake me and He would be my total security.

It all began with a firmly locked door, but Jesus is still opening locked doors today!

Afterword

Years have passed since the events in this book took place and yet the experience of it all is as fresh and real to me as if it happened last week. Jesus has never ceased to be my Lord and Saviour and His joy and love have been an ever-present part of my life. I have had many further adventures with Jesus and fellow Christians at home and abroad and to tell them all would mean another book. Later I met and married my very kind and supportive husband, Mark, and I have had further joy and happiness in our daughters, Judith, Catherine and Michelle. I have known true family happiness, however I never take this for granted because I will not forget that once I had felt trapped and desperate with no hope of true happiness, even though I pretended happiness to my own hurting family.

Is this story still relevant today? Yes, absolutely, because people are still seeking for answers to life's big questions, and because so many religious groups, including The Unification Church (which is even more active now than it was then), are claiming to have the answers.

Millions of people today are aware of a huge emptiness inside, and this includes the many who join a whole variety of religious groups to find the answer but are still faced with life's great eternal question. That's why I believe my particular account is so important, because it was only in Jesus Christ that I found the answer to my questions which filled my aching, empty void.

Yes, there is a God, and He is loving, and He cares about you, and He sent His Son, the one and only Messiah, to die in your place to save you. This is not myth or legend but solid, concrete truth.

Jesus said, 'You shall know the truth, and the truth shall set you free." (John's Gospel 10:36).

I trust and pray that my story and account will be instrumental in your finding faith and freedom in Jesus.

With my love and warmest regards,

In our Saviour the Lord Jesus Christ,

Beth Axton, October 2019

FOR FURTHER INFORMATION AND ADVICE

Cult Information Centre
BCM Cults, London WC1N 3XX
Website: cultinformation.org.uk
Telephone: 07790 753 035

The Family Survival Trust
Website: familysurvivaltrust.org
Tel:0845 6037 121

Appendix

I hope my story will serve as a testimony to the power of the gospel. Despite the fact that a wide variety of organisations claim to reveal the way to God, I have discovered that, "For there is no other name under heaven by which men may be saved, but the name Jesus Christ." (Acts 4:12)

Most of these organisations deny two important facts:

1. The Deity of Jesus Christ and

2. The Salvation gained by the sacrifice and shed blood of Jesus on the cross.

These two points are so important, as the following verses indicate, that I have included some scriptures to enlarge this:

The Deity Of Jesus:

Isaiah 9:6-7

> For unto us a child is born, to us a son is given: and the government will be upon his shoulder, and his name will be called "Wonderful Counsellor, Mighty God, Everlasting Father, Prince of Peace."

Colossians 1:15

> He is the image of the invisible God, the first-born of all creation; for in him all things were created, in heaven and on earth, visible and invisible, whether thrones or dominions or principalities or authorities – all things were created through him and for him. He is before all things, and in him all things hold together. He is the beginning, the first-born from the dead, that in everything he might be pre-eminent. For in him all the fulness of God was pleased to dwell, and through him to reconcile to himself all things, whether on earth or in heaven, making peace by the blood of his cross.

John 14:9

> He who has seen me has seen the Father: how can you say,
> "Show us the Father"? Do you not believe that I am in the
> Father and the Father in me? The words that I say to you I do
> not speak on my own authority; but the Father who dwells in
> me does his works. Believe me that I am in the Father and the
> Father in me.

The Saving Work Of Christ Upon The Cross:

Romans 5:8

> God shows his love for us in that while we were yet sinners
> Christ died for us. Since therefore, we are now justified by his
> blood, how much more shall we be saved by him from the
> wrath of God.

Romans 8:1-4

> There is therefore now no condemnation for those who are in
> Christ Jesus. For the law of the Spirit of life in Christ Jesus has
> set me free from the law of sin and death. For God has done
> what the law .. could not do: sending his own Son in the
> likeness of sinful flesh and as a sin offering, he condemned sin
> in the flesh, in order that the just requirements of the law
> might be fulfilled in us.

2 Corinthians 5:18

> Therefore if anyone is in Christ he is a new creation, the old
> has passed away, behold the new has come. All this is from
> God who through Christ reconciled us to himself and gave us
> the ministry of reconciliation; that is God was in Christ
> reconciling the world to himself, not counting their trespasses
> against them and entrusting to us the message of
> reconciliation. So we are ambassadors for Christ. God is
> making his appeal through us. We beseech you on behalf of
> Christ, be reconciled to God. For our sake he made him to be
> sin who knew no sin so that in him we might become the
> righteousness of God.

Your response

Having read this book and considered all the evidence, take this opportunity to open the door of your life to Jesus Christ today and to enter into His great and loving Salvation:

> **Lord Jesus, Thank you for knocking so patiently on the door of my life and paying the price of sin for me. I ask you to forgive me for all the wrongs I have done and to receive me into the fulness of Your life and kingdom today. Let me experience Your great love and salvation and in Your time baptize me in the Holy Spirit. Let Your deliverance flow through You to me. From this day onwards I start a brand new life in You. Amen.**

If you prayed the above prayer then I know that God will be true to His word and come and dwell within you. At first you take it entirely by faith but soon you will become aware that Jesus is with you wherever you go, gently leading and guiding you through every day. He will never leave you nor forsake you and He will be your greatest friend. He is the One who can open locked doors for you!

John 1:12

> "As many as received Him, to them He gave power to become the sons of God."

Rev 3:20

> "Behold, I stand at the door and knock, and if any one hears my voice, and opens the door, I will come in and abide with him, and he with me."

INVITATION

YOU ARE INVITED TO A ROYAL BANQUET GIVEN BY THE KING OF KINGS

The Pleasure Of Your Company Is Requested

Please Reply

For Your Place Is Not Yet Reserved!

Oh Jesus, You are standing outside the fast closed door,
In lowly patience waiting to pass the threshold o'er:
Shame on us, Christian brethren, His Name and sign who bear;
Oh, shame, three times upon us to keep Him standing there.
Oh Jesus, You are knocking, and lo! that hand is scarred,
And thorns Your brow encircle, and tears Your face have marred:
Oh, love that passes knowledge so patiently to wait!
Oh, sin that has no equal, so fast to bar the gate!
Oh Jesus, You are pleading in accents meek and low;
"I died for you, My children, and will you treat Me so?"
Oh Lord, with shame and sorrow we open now the door:
Dear Saviour, enter, enter, and leave us nevermore.
(William How, 1867)

Out of my bondage, sorrow and night
Jesus, I come! Jesus, I come!
Into Thy freedom, gladness and light
Jesus I come to Thee!

Out of my sickness into Thy health,
Out of my want and into Thy wealth.
Out of my sin and into Thyself,
Jesus, I come to Thee.

Out of my shameful failure and loss,
Jesus, I come! Jesus, I come!
Into the glorious gain of Thy cross,
Jesus I come to Thee!

Out of earth's sorrows into Thy balm,
Out of life's storms and into Thy calm
Out of distress to jubilant psalm,
Jesus, I come to Thee.

Out of unrest and arrogant pride,
Jesus, I come! Jesus, I come!
Into Thy blessed will to abide,
Jesus I come to Thee!

Out of myself to dwell in Thy love,
Out of despair into raptures above,
Upward for aye on wings like a dove,
Jesus, I come to Thee.

Out of the fear and dread of the tomb,
Jesus, I come! Jesus, I come!
Into the joy and light of Thy home,
Jesus I come to Thee!

Out of the depths of ruin untold,
Into the place of Thy sheltering fold.
Ever Thy glorious face to behold,
Jesus, I come to Thee.

(William Sleeper, 1887)

Underwood Free Church, Reading
Mr Sutton of Sutton's Seeds bought the land for the Church

Myself at Culham Laboratories in 1972

Pastor Jim and Janet Morris with their children

Pastor Ben Belsham

My mother, father nd brother Laurie.

40 Hanover Gardens, my first accommodation in London.

St Mark's Vicarage, front and back.

The top of St. Mark's Church, Kennington, where CLC was held.

Nicholas and Marigold Rivett-Carnac.

Christian Life College

Elmer and Jean Darnall
invite you to attend
180 beneficial and edifying nights

Myself with my daughters Judy, Catherine and Michelle, in 1999.

Ena Allwright at 31 Lavendar Gardens, Clapham Common.

Beth with husband, Mark.

We wish you well on your journey.

A Personal Thank You

My grateful thanks go to all those people who asked me to write my story. I always laughingly dismissed the idea thinking that I had no ability to be an author and hoping that if they wished to see it in print that they would write it for me!

However **special thanks** have to go to Timothy Crow who spoke to me seriously about writing it down in my own words and that he would go through it and edit the script. This he did on top of his usual heavy work load and gave me his invaluable help. Without him this book would never have come to print.

Special thanks also have to go to the late Dennis Paterson who published the book with Campaign Literature under the Title of "Opening Locked Doors". When that sold out and went out of print, Freedom Publishing took it on with the title "Why I Left The Moonies" and this remains on Amozan. Now Campaign Literature have printed me a new cover which I hope you will like.

My grateful thanks go to all those who took the time and trouble to write me such appreciative letters. The book also opened the door to many rewarding conversations with others - I loved meeting you all.

Extra Special Thanks go to my loving and kind husband, Mark, who has always shown me his support and encouragement as well as three beautiful daughters in Judith, Catherine and Michelle. God could not have blessed me more than with you as my family.

Printed by Printforce, United Kingdom